DREAMING
GREEN

DREAMING
GREEN

Eco-Fabulous Homes Designed to Inspire

Lisa Sharkey and Paul Gleicher

WITH SARA BLISS

PHOTOGRAPHS BY LINDA BELL HALL

Clarkson Potter/Publishers
New York

Copyright © 2008 by Lisa Sharkey

Published in the United States by Clarkson Potter/Publishers, an imprint of the Crown Publishing Group,
a division of Random House, Inc., New York.
www.crownpublishing.com
www.clarksonpotter.com

CLARKSON POTTER is a trademark and Potter with colophon is a registered trademark of
Random House, Inc.

Library of Congress Cataloging-in-Publication Data
Sharkey, Lisa.
    Dreaming green : eco-fabulous homes designed to inspire / Lisa Sharkey and Paul Gleicher. — 1st ed.
        p.   cm.
    Includes index.
    1. Architecture—Environmental aspects—United States.   2. Architecture, Domestic—United States.
3. Ecological houses—United States.   I. Gleicher, Paul.   II. Title.
NA2542.35.S53 2008
720'.470973—dc22 2007046698

ISBN 978-0-307-39548-1

Printed in China

Design by Lucille Tenazas/Tenazas Design
Photographs by Linda Bell Hall

10 9 8 7 6 5 4 3 2 1

First Edition

This publication uses Forest Stewardship Council (FSC)—certified paper originating
from well-managed forests, controlled and recycled wood or fiber.

To our children:
Greg, Doug, and Casey—
We love you all the way to the moon and back

CONTENTS

9
Introduction

URBAN

15
URBAN PRESERVATION
Sharkey-Gleicher Brownstone
New York, New York

29
NEWLYWED NEST
Dobberfuhl Home
Austin, Texas

41
OCEAN BREEZE
Ennis Residence
Venice Beach, California

55
THE ALLEY BOX
Riili-Worton Home
Seattle, Washington

67
ROYAL RENOVATION
Sinegal Residence
Seattle, Washington

79
PARADISE BY THE SEA
Talib House
Fort Lauderdale, Florida

91
SIDE BY SIDE
Moore-Breedlove and
Anderson-Boyd Duplexes
Austin, Texas

SUBURBAN

103
SIMPLY MODERN
Bennett Family Residence
Easton, Massachusetts

113
SUN HOME
McMurtrie-Service Residence
Ann Arbor, Michigan

123
FROM THE ASHES
Goldberg Family Home
Seattle, Washington

135
CLIFF DWELLERS
Skillman Family Home
San Carlos, California

147
ECOMANOR
Seydel Home
Atlanta, Georgia

RURAL

165
UP IN THE TREETOPS
Johnson-Chronister Home
Austin, Texas

175
EXTRAORDINARY
EXPERIMENT
McDonough-Trang e-House
Stone Ridge, New York

187
RURAL RETREAT
Wente-Hyland Farmhouse
Millerton, New York

203
COUNTRY CHIC
Grier-Steckler Saltbox
Columbia County, New York

215
WOODLAND HIDEAWAY
Hughey-Clancy Residence
Dutchess County, New York

RESOURCES **224**
Acknowledgments **237**
Index **238**

INTRODUCTION

Just five years ago, when our family began a top-to-bottom green renovation of a Manhattan brownstone, it seemed like a completely radical decision. Even though I'm in media and always up on the latest studies and trends, and Paul is an architect, earth-friendly design never seemed like a viable option for us. As city dwellers, it was something we associated with hippie living—picturing far-out houses with roofs made from soda cans, wind generators in the backyard, and lifeless brown hemp fabrics. It took an emotional meeting at an environmental fund-raiser with a couple who built an eco-friendly house after they lost a child to an environmental cancer to make us aware of the link between health and home. As parents of three growing children, we are concerned about the environmental toxins our family is exposed to every day, and we'd introduced organic produce, natural beauty products, and homeopathic medicine into our home. However, we didn't know about the lurking dangers most of us have *inside* our homes. It was frightening to learn that items we all have, such as mattresses, cabinets, and rugs, contain toxic chemicals like flame retardants, formaldehyde, and volatile organic compounds. What's worse is that those chemicals stay in our homes for years, off-gassing into the air we breathe and causing a host of potential health problems that are being linked to diseases such as asthma, cancer, and Alzheimer's.

After that life-changing meeting, Paul and I knew that for the health of our planet, and for our children, we had to go completely green. To be completely honest, though, we didn't know exactly what that would entail; it was literally like stepping into an entirely new world. We can tell you now, however, that it was one of the smartest and best decisions we ever made.

Once we made our green commitment, we set some ground rules—we wanted to try to have almost everything in our house be sustainable or recycled, super energy efficient, and chemical free. And we wanted to source the materials within a 500-mile radius—which is a smart way to lower your carbon footprint by reducing gas and carbon dioxide output. Of course, this was much easier said than done! Finding builders who knew about working this way was a challenge. We found ourselves having to explain what sustainable building was to everyone from our contractor to the painters. It also wasn't an easy road finding resources that fit our style—we wanted our home to feel glamorous and elegant but also family friendly. So we spent dozens of bleary-eyed nights surfing the Web and hours on the phone with experts to track down eco products that fit the bill. The result is an inviting home that's bathed in glowing color and filled with luxurious textures and sophisticated furniture—it doesn't resemble "Birkenstock chic" in the slightest.

The second-floor hallway walls in the Sharkey-Gleicher home are covered in organic clays with golden color and mica chips embedded inside, which gives the home a warm adobe glow. The Lyptus flooring is heavier than oak and is a blend of eucalyptus trees, which grow to full maturity in fifteen years. The stair rail is made from blackened steel, which was manufactured by a local artisan and capped with Lyptus.

The brise-soleil projecting from the floor to ceiling windows shields the rural New York house from the hot summer sun. The operable awning windows allow for fresh air to enter the space.

We decided to write this book to share not only what we've learned but also the experiences of sixteen other daring families who, like us, believe in green living. The houses we chose to feature are not only dialed in to the coolest new eco-friendly alternatives, they are also dazzling in terms of style. From an ultra-sleek house overlooking the Pacific made entirely out of refrigeration panels by superstar eco architect David Hertz, to environmental activist Laura Seydel's grand and elegant, antiques-filled house in Georgia, we found homes to fit every taste.

Throughout this journey, we met many incredibly inspiring homeowners and architects. While some homeowners were ardent environmentalists—like the Bennett family, who dry their laundry outside, ride their bikes to work, and grow their own produce—there were others like Paul Riili, who purchased his eco-home for its industrial chic style but became a convert, filling his place with furniture made from recycled materials like ultra-hip sculptural baskets crafted out of old tires. While there's a common misconception that it costs more to live green, we found houses that fit a range of budgets. Massachusetts-based architect Mary Ann Thompson even designed a home for the Bennett family that was the same cost as a conventional one. The Goldbergs in Seattle and the Skillman family in San Carlos, California, were so committed to building green that they learned how to wire, plumb, and pour concrete so they could build their dream earth-friendly houses within their budget.

What these families have in common is that they are all incredible pioneers. They didn't go the easy route by building green. It would have been a much faster, simpler, and less stressful process for them to just pick out whatever cabinets or flooring or insulation was easily available. But instead they logged in those extra hours, went that extra mile (hopefully on their bikes!), and took the leap of faith that green would be glorious. Because of their hard work, their passion, and their drive, our hope is that you will have an easier time going green. There's more demand out there now for healthy earth-friendly products, and manufacturers large and small are meeting the need with stellar alternatives. We've included a detailed resources section in the back of the book. Whether you're looking for insulation made from recycled newspapers or chemical-free mattresses, we have listed dozens of manufacturers and their contact information so that going green will be a snap.

If you're reading this book because you're exploring living green, there are hundreds of ideas we hope you might consider incorporating into your own home. There are simple changes like using paint that's free of toxic volatile organic compounds or more elaborate transformations like siting your new home to take advantage of passive solar energy. There are also hundreds of stunning design ideas in this book that you may want to incorporate not because they are green but because they are simply beautiful. That's how far eco design has come. We hope that you'll be as moved and inspired by these journeys as we were. We hope that even if you make just a small change in your life, it will be a green one. We believe sustainable design feels great, looks great, and makes an incredible difference.

URBAN

URBAN PRESERVATION

Sharkey-Gleicher Brownstone
New York, New York

EARLY IN THE PROCESS WE DECIDED THAT ALMOST EVERY ASPECT OF THE
RENOVATION WAS GOING TO BE GREEN—FROM THE GUT JOB TO THE DESIGN.
WE WANTED A HEALTHY HOUSE MADE WITH CHEMICAL-FREE, NATURAL
MATERIALS THAT DIDN'T PILLAGE THE EARTH.
—Lisa Sharkey

My husband, Paul, and I have long had a love affair with Manhattan's idyllic Upper West Side. We think the family-friendly neighborhood, with its scenic blocks of charming nineteenth-century brownstones and its easy access to parks and schools, is the perfect place to raise our children, Greg, Doug, and Casey. But finding the town house of our

Above: The open transoms on the parlor floor provide monumental scale and relate to the door beyond, as well as hearken back to the living room windows. Their design helps to widen the brownstone, which is only seventeen feet across. Their thickness gives an intentional appearance of strength and stability. The chest of drawers is by Environment Furniture and is constructed from reclaimed Peroba wood.

Opposite: The living room chairs from Donghia were recovered with postindustrial recycled fabrics by Angela Adams. The console and mirror are made by Environment Furniture from reclaimed wood.

dreams in our beloved neighborhood was challenging. When we started looking five years ago, we knew we needed to find a wreck because that was the only way we could afford a house in our price range, but, boy, did we get one. The four-story c. 1885 home that we purchased had been converted to rental apartments and stripped of all its original character. Thankfully, having an architect in the family has its benefits, and Paul could see beyond the flaws. Knowing he could completely transform the space, we happily prepared ourselves to tackle a major renovation.

Early in the process we decided that almost every aspect of the renovation was going to be green—from the gut job to the design. We

wanted a healthy house made with chemical-free, natural materials. First on the agenda was disposing of hazardous waste properly to avoid contaminating any landfills, so we called in an environmental engineer who helped us remove the asbestos and the leaky oil tanks in the cellar. Next, we saved what we could from the old house, and even items we couldn't use, like warped and cracked wood joists, which we donated to a salvage flooring company. To provide cleaner, more dust-free air quality than forced air, we went with an ultra-efficient boiler and slim-profile radiators.

Aesthetically, we longed for a gorgeous and sophisticated house with rich textures, beautiful shapes, and glorious color that would work for our lively family. Our only worry was whether we could find eco fabrics and furniture that would reflect our style; we had boldly committed to going completely green before we knew for sure what we would find in the design world.

It was, in fact, a much bigger challenge than we anticipated to find suppliers and products that met our green and design standards. For example, we thought it would be simple to find kitchen cabinets that didn't contain formaldehyde and were made from wood certified as being from a sustainable forest. We were able to source them, but we were unable to "find" them locally. So we had to make a concession to our original goal of only buying within a 500-mile radius—and ordered the clean-lined pearwood-veneer cabinets from a supplier in Oregon. We did, however, find one of our favorite eco products, IceStone, just over the bridge in Brooklyn. Our IceStone countertops are just as strong as granite but made from concrete and recycled glass. We selected a luminescent color that features glistening green glass

chips embedded in a polished gray concrete background and paired it with a dazzling mosaic of moss green, blue, and white recycled glass tiles for the backsplash.

We used the leftover IceStone we had for our fireplace surround, as well as for our bathroom counters.

In the spirit of family togetherness, we chose to nix a formal dining room in lieu of having our rectangular dining table and chairs (made from sustainably harvested wood) on one side of the kitchen, with a more casual eat-in semicircular banquette on the other. The kitchen is the center of our household—it's where the kids do homework and hang out with friends, and more often than not, we somehow all make it to the table for dinner, so it made sense to have as many places to lounge, eat, study, and connect as possible. But all that seating, plus the three tall stools that saddle up to the island, required upholstery, which led us to our first round of eco fabric samples. Unfortunately, they all looked and felt like variations on burlap—blah, stiff, and scratchy. Not knowing where else to turn, we hit the trade shows and were lucky to find Angela Adams, a textile designer who specializes in mod, graphic patterns in luscious colors. Angela let us see the very first sample

The recycled fabrics on the banquette show
little dirt and are easy to clean. The glass table
is a family heirloom.

The photos above the dining room table show New York's Central Park in autumn and summer and are by local photographers Ben Packer and Joan Lieber. The dining room table, by Desiron, was selected for its strong rectangular shape and its ability to accommodate large parties for dinner. Desiron's tables are manufactured just across the Hudson River in New Jersey, only a few miles from the brownstone. The bench is intentionally narrow to allow room between two separate eating areas (the dining room table and the kitchen island) in the space.

Above: In the daughter's floral-themed room, the InterfaceFLOR rug is laid down tile-by-tile with sticky corners, to avoid any toxins that can be contained in rug pads or wall-to-wall carpets.

Opposite, above: Homeowner and architect Paul Gleicher designed the master bedroom furniture. It was manufactured by Furnature, a Boston-based company that uses clean, organic, nontoxic materials in its manufacturing process. Lisa's sister Pamelah designed and sewed the pillows from recycled fabrics.

Opposite, below left: The guest bathroom is covered in recycled glass tiles from Oceanside Glass Tile that have an iridescent shimmer.

Opposite, below right: The blue and white Denim Sky IceStone was used on all horizontal surfaces of the master bathroom, including the shower floor. The tub, by Bain Ultra, has a chromatherapy feature, which shines different colored lights into the bath.

of her new green line made from 100 percent recycled fabric. We loved what we saw and ordered a green and pink fabric for our dining chairs and a green trellis pattern for the counter stools. They add a bit of kick to the room we live in most and, because they're made of recycled postindustrial polyester, they are incredibly durable—perfect for chairs that are used 24/7.

Our living room is on the same floor as the kitchen, and the two spaces are connected by an airy stairwell landing that greets visitors as they make their way upstairs from the street-level entry. Defined by a dramatic wall of casement windows that are filled with argon to increase their thermal properties, the light-filled living room captures the very views that drew us to this neighborhood. To take in those views and provide a space for hanging out, we chose a roomy wraparound sectional sofa made without formaldehyde or endangered woods. To give a sense of springtime, we picked fabrics and accessories in soft greens and golden yellows against barely-there soft celery walls. For our floors, we hoped to find a sustainable option other than bamboo, which we worried wasn't durable enough to withstand the hard knocks of two teenage boys, plus our eight-year-old daughter and her friends, and our new puppy, not to mention my high heels. We were thrilled to find Lyptus, a fast-growing renewable hybrid of the eucalyptus tree that is very strong and boasts a rich hue and a striking grain.

Upstairs is Casey's feminine and colorful room; the first thing you notice when you peek inside is her brightly hued FLOR carpet tiles featuring a graphic pattern of yellow, orange, and pink daisies. Her room boasts a wall of casement windows that mimic the ones in the living room. The elegant glass chandelier was

a piece we brought from our old house—it felt too traditional for our living room, but it works perfectly in Casey's sweet room.

The palette in our bedroom, just down the hall, was influenced by the name of the IceStone color we used for our master bathroom—Denim Sky. It inspired me to cover the headboard and the bench at the foot of the bed in soft, durable, organic denim. To keep the space soothing, we went with a palette of dusty blues and creams punctuated by bold fuchsia and denim pillows made of recycled fabrics, hand-sewn by my sister Pamelah. Paul designed all the furniture in our bedroom, and a green furniture manufacturer made the pieces with chemical-free infill and sustainable woods.

Upstairs are the boys' rooms, painted in soft blue and green shades that, like all the paints in the house, contain no volatile organic compounds. Greg and Doug chose their own striped washable FLOR carpet tiles, made from partially recycled materials. For their beds, we found chemical-free mattresses and ultra-soft sheets made of bamboo and beech fibers.

The true gem of the house is the top floor, where you'll find a glass-enclosed room surrounded by a green roof. We were bold with color, choosing a plush orange sofa, which mimics the color of the sunset, and sofas and chairs that are perfect for stargazing. Casey, our youngest, loves to sit up there just as day turns into night and recite "Star Light, Star Bright" when she sees the first star. Our green roof has the added benefit of keeping our house cool and increasing the roof's longevity. It's been said that if everyone in New York had a green roof, the average temperature would drop by as much as five degrees. There are two different types of

The pearwood-veneer cabinets in the kitchen open upward rather than out in order to keep the lines clean in the wide open space. The IceStone countertops are as hard as granite and can withstand both very hot and very cold elements. The glass chips inside sparkle like sea glass and complement the recycled–glass tile backsplash.

green roofs you can choose, and we went with the extensive version, which requires less maintenance and only calls for one inch of soil beneath the plantings. The only downside is that you can't walk on it, so we inserted IceStone pavers that allow you to step between the sedum and not crush the delicate plants. We still find plenty of ways to enjoy our little patch of green, which came with seedlings, flowers, and even crickets. Casey and her friends love to catch crickets and take them to school to feed the frogs, much to the delight of her science teacher, and the sound of crickets chirping outside almost makes us forget that we're in the middle of a bustling city.

This experience has been an incredible adventure for our whole family. Paul was able to educate himself about an entirely new way of building that he can feel good about, and

he's gone on to get his LEED (Leadership in Energy and Environmental Design) accreditation. I love that we've been able to create a beautiful space for our family and that I don't have to worry about the health hazards of anything in our home. As parents, we are so happy that our kids are really seeing firsthand what it means to care about the earth.

People say one person can't make a difference but we really disagree. One person makes a huge impact, and one family even greater impact. Many people are surprised to learn our house is green, and that's exactly the compliment that we hoped for. We want our house to prove that being green doesn't mean you have to sacrifice style. You can create a beautiful home that takes little from the earth and gives back to you in countless ways.

Above left: The copper pot beneath the powder-room sink was hand-tooled by Lisa Sharkey's great-grandfather at the turn of the twentieth century. The artwork is by Yuri Gorbachev, cousin of former Soviet president Mikhail Gorbachev. The vanity is a Lefroy Brooks Double Iroko Hardwood table. The bathroom fixtures are designed to store water and prevent scalding.

Above right: The eco fireplace is specifically designed for a maximum amount of heat to stay inside the living room. The extremely shallow depth of the fireplace forced the heat into the room and minimizes the amount that can escape into the chimney.

Below left: IceStone is made of recycled glass and concrete; it's seen here in Sage Pearl. The factory is in Brooklyn, just a subway ride from the Green Brownstone.

Below right: Oceanside Glass Tile is also made of recycled glass. The company uses more than six hundred tons of recycled glass bottles every year in their manufacturing process.

Bottom: Imagine Tiles are made in a process that uses recycled water.

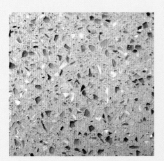

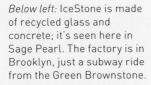

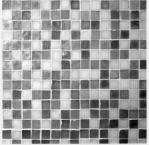

1. WHOLE HOUSE WATER FILTRATION SYSTEM
   All the water that enters our house is filtered via an EcoWater filtration system located in the cellar. The system removes at least 95 percent of the impurities in the water and softens it as well.

2. HIGH-EFFICIENCY BOILER
   Our ultra-efficient boiler burns 98 percent of the gas (only 2 percent wasted), saving energy and fuel costs.

3. RADIATORS
   Rather than rely on forced air, which produces dust, mold spores, and other allergens, we chose to install radiators throughout. Myson radiators come in a sleek modern design and have a slim profile.

4. GREEN ROOF
   Our green roof helps to keep the house cool in the summer, which reduces energy costs. It also increases the longevity of the roof below and absorbs 80 percent of the rainfall that otherwise ends up in the city sewage system.

5. CLAY WALLS
   Clay walls in the stairwells and on the ground floor are natural and nontoxic. They "breathe," pulling in the humidity and keeping the house cool.

6. LYPTUS FLOORS
   A hybrid of two eucalyptus trees, Lyptus is grown in managed forests in Brazil and matures in fourteen to sixteen years, compared to eighty years for many hardwoods. It has a strength and density similar to maple.

7. ICESTONE
   IceStone is available in twenty-seven colors. It is heat resistant, as strong as granite, and free of VOCs (volatile organic compounds).

8. GLASS TILE BACKSPLASH
   Made from recycled glass bottles and silica sand, these square tiles are beautiful, durable, and waterproof.

9. RECYCLED FABRICS
   Angela Adams's colorful patterned fabrics in the kitchen and livng room were made from 100 percent postindustrial recycled fabrics.

10. SUSTAINABLE FURNITURE
    All of the new furniture in the house was produced without formaldehyde, chemicals, dyes, polymers, or toxins. Some pieces use reclaimed wood, while others use wood that is sustainably harvested.

NEWLYWED NEST

Dobberfuhl Home
Austin, Texas

WHAT'S GREAT IS A LOT OF PEOPLE OUR AGE GREW UP LEARNING ABOUT
THE IMPORTANCE OF BEING KIND TO THE EARTH, SO NOW WE ARE APPLYING
THAT INFORMATION AS ADULTS.
— Chris Cobb, project architect

Preceding pages, left: Redwood walls echo the home's woodsy exterior. The natural materials used in accent pieces increase the organic beauty of the couple's living room.

Preceding pages, right: The owners couldn't bear to cut down the gigantic old oak tree, so they built the house around it. Now a centerpiece of the home, it provides shade from the hot Austin sun.

Opposite: The rainwater empties off of the entryway canopy and is collected in the basin below, then used to water the plants.

Above: The airy, open design of the space keeps the total square footage down, to save energy costs and decrease the carbon footprint.

Dr. Steven Dobberfuhl has been planning to build an eco-friendly house since the fourth grade. All throughout grade school, Steven and his best friend, Chris Cobb, now an architect, spent recess sketching out ideas for their future houses. Growing up in Austin, Texas, an eco-progressive town, was a big influence on their environmental know-how, so even in those early years building green was always part of the plan. "We imagined a house that glorified the idea of living with nature," Steven explains. "We had big ideas to live off the grid, generating our own power from windmills, solar panels, or even water turbines."

Cut to twenty-five years later, when Steven returned to Austin to set up his internal medicine practice. After spending time traveling and finishing medical school, he was ready to put down roots in his hometown and, after decades of free consultations, to hire Chris officially. After a year of searching (with Chris advising him, of course), Steven found a scenic tree-filled lot just a block away from Austin's hip SoCo district that's bustling with shops and restaurants. He was drawn to the wooded property that was just minutes away from the lively downtown scene.

The site's biggest challenge was also one of its greatest assets, a gorgeous forty-foot oak tree stood smack in the center of the buildable section of the property. "The design arose from the need to build in relation to the tree," explains Chris. "We didn't want to create some big boring box that just sat in

front of it." Instead, Chris's design features a dynamic interplay of different heights and geometries that interact beautifully with the tree, literally tucking the house under one of its larger branches. Adding even more shade is a tall elm tree that frames the opposite side of the house. To make sure the structure blended rather than contrasted with the landscape, they chose massaranduba, a Brazilian redwood siding for the exterior. To blur the line between indoors and out, Chris crafted several interior walls out of the same redwood planks. Deep chocolate bamboo floors meld beautifully with the reddish shade of the wood walls. While the style of the house is contemporary, the wood softens all the angles and visually connects the house to the tree-filled lot.

Steven had two main requests of Chris's design. First, it was imperative that the design be green—already a specialty of Chris's practice. "I just think practicing sustainable architecture is part of being a good architect," Chris says. So the first step was to keep the house small to limit its environmental as well

as visual impact. "We wanted it to fit with the neighborhood in terms of scale; I didn't want a modern McMansion," admits Steven. The size was kept to 2,200 square feet, in keeping with the midsize century-old homes that line the block.

One of the things Steven likes best about the house is its energy efficiency. "I'm cheap!" He laughs. "I went green to avoid high bills." Steven estimates that his friends with similar-sized homes spend about $200 to $300 monthly on electricity while he pays $90 on average. The reason for the sharp contrast is due primarily to the structurally insulated panels that were used for all exterior walls.

The house is so cool that even in the hot Texas summers, he rarely has to use air-conditioning. Instead, ceiling fans and a well-designed ventilation system keeps cooled air circulating.

Steven's second request was for versatility. He needed a flexible space that would work as well for his life as a bachelor as when he married and had children. Chris's solution was to create one bedroom upstairs, with the

Above: The suspended kitchen shelf above the granite countertops complements the room's open design.

Opposite: Light peeks through the master bath, warming up the cool colors of the tile.

Left: Doorways without moldings save wood during construction. Their metal frames finish off the simple design.

Below and opposite: The bright orange chairs in the couple's home were purchased from a local vintage shop to spice up the color palette of earth tones.

ability to convert an office area into another bedroom. On the first floor Chris designed an open layout plan that features living, dining, and kitchen areas that all flow into one another, for a space that works as well for a cocktail party as it will for playing with kids. The masculine open kitchen is the heart of the house and features crisp birch cabinets and dark granite countertops. A suspended shelf, which echoes and reinforces the open rectangular shape of the kitchen, displays decorative bowls from Steven's volunteering trips to South America.

By the time the framing of the house was complete, in March 2006, it was apparent that he and Chris were wise to think ahead and imagine a family living there. Steven was in the midst of a whirlwind courtship of Becca Bruce, and very quickly priorities changed as Steven envisioned Becca living with him in his

new place. Five months later they were engaged and Becca moved in. But while Becca and Steven are the perfect match romantically, designwise they had their differences. Becca grew up in a house full of color, fabrics, and antiques; modern design was never in her visual vocabulary. Steven prefers minimal furnishings, no pattern, and a clean pale palette. For example, he doesn't have curtains. "People can't look in, so we don't need them," he explains practically about the upstairs rooms. But for Becca this superminimal style was a big change. "I had an aversion to modern." Becca laughs. "I was worried it wasn't going to be comfortable or warm."

Because they were still dating when Steven was picking out furnishings, Becca was hesitant to put too much of her stamp on the interior. When he chose a low-profile wood

The bedroom is simple and soothing. The nook above the couple's queen-sized bed is perfect for displaying art objects.

Right: The frosted sliding glass panels above the counter-tops conceal products yet leave them easily accessible.

Bottom right: An old pecan tree is given a new life as open shelving in the light-filled foyer.

The giant windows in the dining nook create the feeling of actually eating outdoors.

bed with two individual headrests and only added a wood chair and pale green sheets, she didn't interfere. She even approved the buttery yellow sectional and two chocolate suede armchairs for the living room. However, when Steven started looking at glass and steel coffee tables, she stepped in. "I told him he needed something softer," she states. "They aren't the most child-friendly materials!" Together the couple found a pretty brown wood coffee table from a local furnituremaker just around the corner. And Becca was right: the durable surface stands up to their friends' toddlers. "The house is perfect for kids," says Becca, who keeps one closet full of toys for younger guests. "The flow is circular around the kitchen and there are always children running around."

When Becca moved in, she didn't bring a lot with her, just an octagonal antique table from home and a painting of the Green Mountains of Vermont. She'd discovered that so many of her old pieces just didn't work with the home's unique style. "What's so interesting is how the design of a house dictates how you live," she says. "The clean lines of this place force you to live a simpler life with less clutter." The architecture also calls out for geometric furniture that Becca has learned to

love. "I work from home. I love how serene and calm it is in here so I can really focus." Now that they're married, Becca has started adding her own touches. For a jolt of color, they recently purchased a pair of vintage orange chairs, one of which was just what was needed to brighten and soften up their bedroom. Plus, her favorite hue was incorporated into the master bath in the form of fluffy orange towels. "I'm dying to add more color," Becca says, staring at the white walls. Steven is quick to agree. "I really would like to see more color," he says. "We're ready to paint!"

For the happy couple, the most surprising thing about living in their sustainable house is how normal it feels. "I certainly don't feel like I've made any sacrifices," Steven says. "There are all these green components to the house that only make it better." Becca, a consultant for nonprofit organizations that build low-income housing, is proud to be able to share her new green knowledge to inspire her clients. But the best part comes from how connected they feel to nature every day. "We wake up every morning and I look up into the oak tree through our window and I just feel like we're living at the top of this tree," says Steven. It sounds just like one of the amazing green ideas he envisioned years ago.

Top left: The countertops are made of honed black granite, but without the final layers of polish, to achieve a textured, dull service. In certain granites, however, honing eliminates patterns and colors on the surface and makes cleaning more difficult.

Top right: The recycled steel siding develops a natural rusted patina, which helps unify the exterior of the house's horizontal Brazilian redwood with the surrounding wooden landscape.

Above: Although saving this tree cost more than losing it, it adds to the home's intrigue—and greenness.

1. **CELLULOSE INSULATION**
Cellulose insulation, made primarily from recycled newspapers, is highly efficient, sealing the home against air infiltration to maximize energy efficiency.

2. **MARMOLEUM FLOORS**
Marmoleum flooring is made from natural raw materials, including linseed oil, rosins, and wood flour with a natural jute backing. It's installed with solvent-free adhesives and no VOCs.

3. **GEOTHERMAL HEATING**
Geothermal heat pumps use the stable 51 degrees F. of the ground to provide heating and cooling to the house. In the winter, using geothermal heat reduces bills by more than 50 percent of what they would be with a propane furnace. In the summer, geothermal cooling keeps the house cool for a third less than conventional central air-conditioning systems.

4. **RAINWATER COLLECTION**
Rainwater is collected in large cisterns and used for flushing the toilets and irrigating the landscape.

5. **GRAY WATER SYSTEM**
Dish, shower, sink, and laundry water (gray water) is reused for watering the plants and lawn.

6. **COMPUTER-CONTROLLED ENERGY SYSTEMS**
A touch-screen computer system controls all the major systems in the house, including entertainment, security, communications, water collection, lighting, and climate control. Energy and water usage are observable and controlled up to the minute.

7. **DOORS**
The Humabuilt Wheatcore interior doors have cores made of rapidly renewable resources with wood veneer exteriors. They are FSC certified, use ultra-low-VOC water-based adhesives, and contain no formaldehyde.

8. **TUBULAR SKYLIGHTS**
Solar tubes from the roof allow light to reach into interior closets and bathrooms that don't have windows. The glass used in the skylights and tubing blocks all infrared heat and fade-causing UV rays, while letting in abundant natural light.

9. **NATURAL FABRICS**
Only 100 percent natural fabrics without chemical treatments were used for upholstery, bedding, and curtains. Fabrics in either cotton, silk, wool, linen, jute, and hemp were used throughout.

10. **RECYCLED-CONTENT COUNTERS**
Eco-friendly countertops made from concrete mixed with recycled materials, including mother-of-pearl, glass, and marble, are a gorgeous and strong alternative to quarried stone.

OCEAN BREEZE

Ennis Residence
Venice Beach, California

EVEN WHEN INSIDE, YOU FEEL AS IF YOU'RE A PART OF THE BEACH—THE OCEAN IS
AN EXTENSION OF WHATEVER ROOM YOU'RE IN. LOOKING AT THE HOUSE FROM THE SAND,
THE BUILDING DISPLAYS A MIRROR REFLECTION OF THE PALM TREES AND THE SURF,
LITERALLY MARRYING THE BEACH WITH THE STRUCTURE.

—Thomas Ennis

Previous pages, left: The prefabricated industrial panels used to construct the house took only a week to assemble.

Previous pages, right: Lounge chairs atop the Pacific coastline beach house allow for ultimate views of the ocean by day and the stars by night.

Thomas Ennis wasn't looking to live in a green house. In 2003 all he really wanted was a stunningly designed home that would stand out from the beachfront houses that line Venice Beach in California. For his narrow 28 x 89-foot lot mere inches from the sand, Thomas, the owner of a commercial car-wash manufacturing business, dreamed of something eye-catching that would reflect his cutting-edge style. "I'm an inventor," he explains. "I love high-tech everything; I didn't want the same old thing."

While he was on the hunt for an architect to fulfill his vision, he noticed local design star David Hertz's own McKinley house, just a few blocks away. When he checked out David's show-stopping contemporary twist on Balinese style, he knew he had found the right man for the job. What Thomas didn't know was that David, a former protégé of Frank Gehry, has long been an eco pioneer, building sustainable, energy-efficient homes that also push aesthetic boundaries, such as the house he built from an abandoned 747 jumbo jet. "I went to architecture school in the seventies, during the energy crisis in California," says David. "I'm also a lover of being in nature, so environmental activism is a core part of my work."

David, a native Californian, frequently surfs right in front of Thomas's lot, so he knew the landscape well from both land and sea. When the two met, Thomas had a definitive sense of what he liked and disliked. "I wanted a house built of concrete, metal, and glass." No wood because of termites and rot. No stucco because it's messy. "I had a stucco house and I don't think I ever got it completely off the outside windows." And brick and mortar is a look he's simply not partial to. Aesthetically, he was looking for a statement. "He wanted it to be a showpiece," says David.

David granted all of Thomas's wishes in a dramatic design that also incorporates a plethora of energy-saving features and materials. David's design utilized steel, glass, and concrete, but added a visionary twist with prefabricated 30-inch wide and 30-foot tall panels. Each preassembled panel, typically used for commercial walk-in refrigeration units, has a 6-inch foam core, clad in sheets of aluminum and finished with a marine paint finish resistant to sun, sand, and salt. "I was fascinated with the idea that a wall could be a complete unit encompassing the structure, the insulation, the exterior, and the interior all at once," explains David. The off-the-shelf prefabricated material has the added advantage of being easy to assemble, knocking months off construction time. The lightweight panels simply interlock together to form the exterior. The total time for two men to construct the exterior? Only one week. Another bonus to using the panels was saving trees because no framing was needed. "With a prefab wall you minimize the drywall, paint, stucco, framing, and scaffolding, which significantly reduces construction waste," David points out.

While Thomas was excited about the green components of the house, like the rooftop photovoltaic panels that provide the house with most of its energy needs, he almost drew the line when David told him that they wouldn't need to install air-conditioning. "It was an uphill fight for David," remembers Thomas, who was skeptical that he wouldn't need AC at all. It took a lot of coaxing to prove that a combination of factors would maximize the ocean breezes, keeping the house cool even on the hottest days. "A building made of these panels could keep ice frozen in the desert," David tells us. Because the panels also

The living room is sited toward the ocean. The couch was custom-designed to keep from obstructing the view. The suspended chair is a favorite spot for reading, meditating, or simply watching the waves.

Opposite: The glass roof allows sunlight to stream down the stairs, landing on the dining room table.

Above: One-way glass windows allow people to see out during the day but prevent passersby from peeking inside. Curtains maintain nighttime privacy.

Left: The master bath is part of the bedroom.

eliminate the need for load-bearing walls, the interior of the three-story structure is primarily open, allowing natural ventilation to flow freely through the house. "I skewed the outside walls so they act like gills to funnel air flow," says David. If it does get to 82 degrees inside, the thermostat-controlled skylights are programmed to open, letting the hot air out. Plus, even with an abundance of west-facing glass, a reflective solar film blocks out the sun (and prying eyes from the beach). "I don't miss air-conditioning at all," says Thomas.

Thomas, a single father, whose children, Jack, eleven, and Savannah, thirteen, enjoy the house part-time, wanted the interior of the house to reflect the sleek sensibility of the architecture but remain kid-, guest-, and beach-friendly—a tall order. To help put it all together, Thomas sought the help of Joe Lucas and Parrish Chilcoat of Lucas Studio. "Thomas told us he wanted the house to be bulletproof," says Parrish. "Making it user-friendly but still very contemporary was our assignment." Thomas concurs. "I told them it's a beach home, it's going to have a lot of sand and a lot of kids. I don't want there to be anyplace they can't go." Joe and Parrish's solution was to fill the space with durable, long-wearing materials that could stand up to sand, salt water, and the occasional spill. The curtains in the bedrooms are made from an outdoor fabric that won't fade, and the carpets are an industrial quality that will last for decades. The brown swivel armchairs in the living room are slipcovered in a durable cotton that can go right in the wash. And the boxy sofa is upholstered in a 100 percent polyester fabric that mimics the look and feel of Ultra-suede but won't absorb spills. For Thomas, who loves to entertain, the polished concrete

floors are the ideal material. "They're inde-structible," he says. "I can have a party and not worry about anyone spilling red wine."

To work with the gray concrete floors and gray panel walls, Joe and Parrish went with a masculine palette of creams, muted greens, and browns. They chose modern furniture that's sleek and sexy but also comfortable—curved white swivel chairs that saddle up to the kitchen counter, a faded brown leather bed frame, and boxy modern sofas. Against the gray backdrop, the effect is very James Bond, a manly yet sophisticated interior. But by choosing welcoming, comfy sofas and chairs, and playful pieces like a Lucite egg chair on the terrace and the green shag carpet in Savannah's room, it's more like James Bond with kids.

Thomas's love of invention and new ideas is in evidence throughout the house. Push a button and the huge 9 x 15-foot living room window drops down to just three feet above the floor, leaving the whole room open to the beach. "I had so many crazy ideas like that window, and David would always say 'great idea, let's make that happen,'" says Thomas.

The house plays up its relationship to the beach, with ocean views from every room. Even when you're inside, you feel as if you're a part of the beach. Looking at the house from the sand, the building displays a mirror reflection of the palm trees and the surf, literally marrying the beach with the structure. The effect is breathtaking. But the relationship goes both ways, much to Thomas's delight. "I never fail to look out and see someone admiring the house or taking a photo of it," he says. "It gives back to the neighborhood a place for everyone to enjoy. It's a part of Venice."

Individual monopoints of light are suspended from the exposed structural steel frame of the house and surround the floating white ceiling at the center of the room.

The wood in the kitchen softens the room and contrasts with the other materials, which include metal, glass, and concrete. The house is designed to force rising heat through the staircase and out of the skylights, which open automatically with temperature sensors.

Lunch guests are showered with light from above
as they dine at the natural-wood dining table.

The floor-to-ceiling living room windows are
mounted on a motorized gear system that lowers
them into the basement, allowing fresh air to fill
this unair-conditioned home.

1. **PANELS**
   Prefabricated refrigeration panels with a high insulation value were used for the exterior walls. The panels eliminate the need for wood framing and additional insulation, and reduce the home's energy needs.

2. **PHOTOVOLTAIC PANELS**
   Fourteen south-facing PV panels produce 2.3 kilowatts of energy per day, often sending excess electricity back to the grid.

3. **SOLAR COLLECTORS**
   Solar hydronic radiant heating panels on the roof convert the sun's warmth to heat the home's water.

4. **RADIANT-HEAT FLOORING**
   Two zones on each floor allow for targeted heating on cool evenings. Hot water provided by solar collectors on the roof run underneath concrete floors that evenly conduct the heat.

5. **ULTRA-EFFICIENT BOILER**
   An energy-efficient boiler provides additional hot water when needed with an extremely efficient boiler that burns 98 percent of the gas (wasting only 2 percent).

6. **PEX TUBING**
   Instead of copper tubing that can leach minerals into the water, Thomas chose plastic PEX tubing, which delivers water of better quality and purity.

7. **SMART GLASS**
   All the windows on the front, west-facing side of the house are laminated with a reflective solar film and low-E coating, which provides privacy and limits the UV rays and heat that enter the house.

8. **THERMOSTATICALLY CONTROLLED SKYLIGHTS**
   When the temperature inside the house gets above 82 degrees, the skylights are set to automatically open to allow the warm air to escape.

9. **FSC-CERTIFIED WALNUT CABINETRY**
   The kitchen and bathroom cabinets and countertops are made of walnut from a Forest Stewardship Council–certified sustainable growth forest.

10. **PNEUMATIC ELEVATOR**
    Because Thomas's mother often visits, it's helpful to have an elevator for her to navigate the 4,000-square-foot house. The glass elevator operates without cables or pulleys. Air pressure from pumps and vacuums push and pull the elevator between the four stories.

Above: The X-shaped steel beams above the pool support the house.

Below: The homeowner designed the unique gas fire, which burns through metal slivers for a dramatic effect.

THE ALLEY BOX

Riili-Worton Home
Seattle, Washington

I LOVE THAT THERE'S A STORY BEHIND EVERYTHING IN THIS HOUSE. IT INSPIRES
PEOPLE TO THINK TWICE ABOUT THE PROJECTS THAT THEY'RE DOING AND LOOK INTO
RECYCLED OR SUSTAINABLE MATERIALS. THEY LOOK AT SOMETHING AND THINK, "I
MIGHT TRY THAT, IT'S A COOL IDEA."
— Paul Riili

Most days, hardly any traffic goes by Paul Riili and Clint Worton's house located off a very quiet alley in Seattle's Madison Valley neighborhood. But occasionally someone will take a wrong turn and inadvertently drive down their narrow street. It only takes a few seconds before Paul and Clint notice the car suddenly stopping in front of their ultracontemporary house. "We laugh," says Paul, an IT director for Expedia. "The house is such a totally different look for the neighborhood, people just jam on their brakes when they see it."

It was originally built as a spec house by local eco builder Jim Barger, of Greenleaf Construction. Built on a lot that was zoned for four houses, Jim put in only three so each would have a yard. He gave the two street-facing homes traditional features like roomy front porches and gabled roofs to fit in with the neighborhood's 1930s Craftsman homes. But for the alley house that's hidden from the street, Jim wanted something entirely unexpected, to surprise whoever happens upon it. For that he turned to husband-and-wife architecture team Kim Lavacot and David Bennett of Browning Lowe Ashdown (BLA) Architects.

Kim and David's design for the 1,400-square-foot alley house didn't disappoint. Inspired by the look of commercial properties, the dark gray structure is enlivened by a peekaboo corner of painted silver siding, graphic window groupings, and a cheery aqua door frame that beckons you inside. "It doesn't look like any house I've ever seen," says Clint. "And I love that." For the interior, the architects went with the theme of "structure as finish"— when you walk into the house you immediately notice that everything is exposed, from the air ducts to the ceiling joists—for a strong dose of industrial chic. Individual lightbulbs hang down from the ceiling beams, concrete floors are underfoot, and the wood ceiling was salvaged from the deconstruction of a local cabinet shop. "We have friends over at least three times a week," says Clint as they prepare lunch in the kitchen that opens to the living and dining area. Adds Paul, "They're amazed by the cool open look. It's just a space everyone wants to hang out in."

Because Paul and Clint spend most weekends entertaining, the open kitchen works perfectly. Stop by on a Saturday and you're likely to find the couple and three or four friends all preparing different courses at once. For Paul, it's reminiscent of childhood parties where dozens of his Italian relatives and friends gathered and cooked together. "It's the same but without the arguing." He laughs, adding, "In this space, there's just positive energy all around."

Because the architecture required understated modern furniture, Paul worked with a close friend, designer Jonathan Mathews of the Kwanchai design firm, to pull it all together, using the move as an excuse to start fresh in the design. "I previously lived with tons of Victorian, Edwardian-looking stuff, so this is a nice change," says Paul. The only piece he couldn't part with was a tall nineteenth-century grandfather clock that he bought as a birthday present for himself. For the living space, his designer chose large pieces with clean lines that do double duty in keeping the space flexible for dinners, parties, or kicking back. A square leather ottoman works as seating or as a place to rest a tray filled with hors d'oeuvres. The salvaged wood pedestal is a side table or a stool, and the sofa made by West Elm doubles as an extra bed for guests. The materials and tones were chosen to echo the interior architectural elements—the metal

dining chairs pick up the silver hue of the ducts, the beige and gray carpet squares mimic the look and tones of the concrete floor, and the bamboo table echoes the warm honey shade of the wood ceiling.

To punctuate the neutral palette of grays, browns, and whites, the couple injected a few pops of intense color. An apple green wall defines the foyer and extends to the second floor, warming up a corner of the bedroom. The bathroom area was a happy aqua and orange. "I wanted the house to feel bright," Paul says.

Upstairs the couple went with a Zen vibe. "The rest of the house is for entertaining, but upstairs is our space," explains Paul. "It's a calm area where we can just chill and relax." They achieved the laid-back aura with minimal furniture, a soft palette, and plenty of pillows. A custom dark-stained oversized wood headboard was cut to the same width as the rectangular window above and provides a focal point for the space. A wool rug is layered over the wall-to-wall carpet, defining a lounging area peppered with silk embroidered bolsters and floor pillows.

But when guests first visit, it's not only the funky modern furniture or bursts of color that have people talking, it's also the eco aspects that spark their curiosity. "I love that there's a story behind everything in this house," Paul says. "It inspires people to think twice about the projects that they're doing and look into recycled or sustainable materials. They look at something and think, 'I might try that; it's a cool idea.'"

Paul and Clint like to share the story of their home's green journey with guests. In 2002, Jim, the home's builder, had a terrifying reaction to a toxic floor finish. After just a few hours of breathing in the fumes, he landed in the emergency room, unable to see straight. His pulse dropped alarmingly low and he lost feeling in his head and mouth due to loss of blood flow to the brain. It took him nine months to fully recover. While he was on the mend, Jim studied everything he could about the health hazards of chemicals in building materials, finishes, and paints that he frequently came into contact with. "The whole experience made me think, What am I exposing my employees to? What's happening to my home buyers who have these materials offgassing in their homes?" Jim reveals. He decided from then on to green-certify every single job. "I feel so good when I walk through a house with a customer and I'm not afraid of what they are breathing in."

For Paul, who was initially attracted to the home's cool design, the walk-through with Jim was eye-opening. "The green parts of the house became significant to me," Paul tells us. "I didn't know a lot about green building before this house." So when it came time to make the house his own visually, Paul made sure to include green components in the interior design. The aluminum dining chairs are crafted from metal salvaged from a Boeing jet. The dining table is sustainable bamboo. His favorite eco-chic pieces are three large black rubber vases made from recycled tires. "We accumulate so many tires in landfills, it's such a cool idea to use them as a design piece," muses Paul. "Living here has opened my eyes."

Above: The kitchen cabinets are made from plywood, not particle board, and are constructed without formaldehyde.

Far left: These containers are recycled tires and are modeled after early leather originals.

Left: The door that opens onto the stone patio provides cross-ventilation for the house, eliminating the need for air-conditioning.

Above: The bathroom cabinets were treated with a water-based finish. The open shelving in the vanity conserves wood and allows easy access to clean towels.

Right: The bedroom is in a loft space that opens onto the downstairs to maximize light and create a calming environment.

The bifold door was chosen because when open it does not project too far into the bedroom. The platform bed allows air to circulate and the Chinese bamboo plants on the bedside table are said to bring prosperity into the home.

The interior staircase was crafted with extra pieces of wood from the local lumber supplier.

The oversized floor pillows are perfect for lounging and watching television in this relaxed, casual room of earth tones. Using large-scale pillows as furniture keeps the space from becoming overcrowded and makes it easy to rearrange for guests, while keeping the view to the outside unobstructed.

GREEN FEATURES

1. **SALVAGED STRUCTURAL LUMBER**
   Most of the wood used to frame the house was salvaged.

2. **PASSIVE SOLAR**
   The architects chose to orient most of the windows facing east, for morning sun, and south, to warm up the house in the winter. The concrete floors act as a thermal mass, retaining heat during the day.

3. **JOB-SITE RECYCLING**
   Eighty-seven percent of postconstruction materials were recycled.

4. **SALVAGED BRICK**
   The exterior staircase gave new life to salvaged bricks.

5. **NO AC**
   With well-placed windows on opposite sides of the boxy house, the house gets enough cross-ventilation to eliminate the need for air-conditioning.

6. **ENGINEERED WOOD STAIRCASE**
   The interior staircase was crafted with scraps from the lumber supplier.

7. **SALVAGED CEILING**
   The ceiling of the living/dining/kitchen area was salvaged from a local cabinet shop.

8. **ECO-KITCHEN CABINETS**
   The cabinets are made of nonformaldehyde plywood, not particleboard, so there is no off-gassing.

9. **LOW-VOC PAINTS**
   Paints without volatile organic chemicals were used throughout.

10. **WATER-BASED WOOD FINISHES**
    Water-based finishes to treat wood cabinets and stair treads are a safer alternative than oil-based.

Far left: The ceiling is made from salvaged wood. Contacting a local cabinetmaker can be an easy and inexpensive way to source reclaimed wood materials.

Above right: The reclaimed brick used as the backsplash in the kitchen has an old-world feel and adds a sense of history to this modern, industry-inflected home.

Left: The industrial chic suspended bulb hangs above the kitchen table.

ROYAL RENOVATION

Sinegal Residence
Seattle, Washington

I REALLY HAD A VISION FOR THE HOUSE. I WANTED THE MOLDING AND FLOORS TO BE
TRUE TO THE ORIGINAL CHARACTER BUT THE INTERIOR TO BE CONTEMPORARY.

— David Sinegal

"I immediately had a vision for this house," explains David Sinegal about the stunning 1910 colonial in Seattle he spent two and a half years eco-renovating. "I wanted all the moldings and flooring to be true to the original character of the house, but the interior design to be very contemporary."

When David first laid eyes on the charming property, it was in bad shape, having suffered through a variety of poorly thought-out renovations that left it with a choppy layout, outdated fixtures, and a frightening avocado green kitchen. But David saw its potential. "It had great bones," he explains, and a cavernous, unfinished 1,100-square-foot attic where he could add more bedrooms to the home's existing three, a major plus, since he has three children who live with him part-time—Jessica, nineteen; Victoria, fifteen; and David Jr., ten. But what closed the deal were the postcard-worthy views in every direction. Located at the top of Queen Anne Hill, the house boasts to-die-for vistas of Mount Rainier, the Seattle skyline, the Olympic mountain range, and Elliott Bay.

To transform the place to its original glory and then some, David turned to local architect Stuart Silk. Initially the plan was just to turn the attic space into three extra bedrooms and two baths, fix up the exterior, and knock down a few walls to expand a couple of rooms. "That quickly became phase one," David says, laughing. Phase two was conceived almost immediately afterward, turning the unfinished basement into a sleek hangout zone complete with a theater room, a small gym, another bedroom and a wet bar. And while he was in the thick of it, he thought, why not add a phase three? Renovations were going so well he couldn't overlook the kitchen—a cramped, awkward space with barely enough room for two people, let alone his whole family. He

envisioned a more fluid space with an additional sunroom. The avocado green cabinets, outdated appliances, and sponge-painted walls were desperately in need of a makeover. "The kitchen was an example of what a bad design era the seventies were."

Stuart, a veteran architect, brought to the table not only decades of experience but a deeply rooted knowledge of sustainable design. David says, "In terms of green living, I knew it was important to be conscious of your imprint on the earth, but it was largely through Stuart's recommendations that I really learned about how to do something about it." Stuart steered David toward more sustainable choices, both small and large—from outfitting all the light fixtures with compact fluorescents to mimicking the hip look of wengé, a threatened exotic tropical hardwood, by adding a dark stain to locally grown certified sustainable white oak.

For David's house, the firm ensured that every aspect of the renovation, starting with the demolition, was up to their high eco standards. They sent everything that could possibly be reused to an architectural salvage yard, from old sinks and appliances to doorknobs. To avoid contaminating a landfill with hazardous waste, toxic materials like antifreeze from the construction trucks and oil from the old boiler were disposed of at an oil disposal facility. And the firm saved every scrap of material that could possibly be recycled.

While older homes are often challenging to retrofit green because they are notorious energy wasters, Silk brought the house up to his high energy standards with a few clever solutions. Rather then tear down walls to reinsulate them, he drilled small holes and blew in insulation. Old leaky windows were replaced with airtight ones and additional windows

This glamorous yet approachable living room is decorated in all-natural textures, such as chenille and velvet. The unusual back-to-back sofa configuration works in this large room as one sofa faces the fireplace and another faces out to the view.

The sweeping and classic center hall Colonial staircase is further enhanced by semigloss white paint that highlights the elegant architectural details. The bright front door and glass sidelights are offset nicely by the dark wood floors. The recessed panels of the newel post and the front door complement the entryway moldings.

were added to bring in more light during the day and provide cross-ventilation, which is given a boost by a new whole-house fan.

Like most renovations, this one had its share of unwelcome surprises. Dry rot, structural issues, awkwardly placed beams, and an ancient electrical system all added to the challenge of remodeling the old building. "Every time you do anything to a one-hundred-ten-year-old house a lot of unknown issues are going to come up," says David. One of the worst bombshells was that there wasn't enough water pressure to reach the new third-floor bathrooms because the floor is higher than the local water tower. But though the snag required a pressure booster and another go-round with the plumbing, the reason behind it was a pleasant shock—it turned out that David's house is actually the highest point in all of Seattle. "I had no idea," says David.

After two and a half years of renovating, when it finally came time to outfit the interiors, David turned to designer Jeff Eckmann, who infused the expansive house with a major shot of glamour. His recipe for elegant yet cool style involved neutral walls in various shades of gray and bright white paint to highlight the period moldings and architectural details. The furniture was chosen for its sophisticated silhouettes and covered in rich chenilles, velvets, and soft cottons. The grand entrance hall boasts ten-foot-high ceilings, and the original oak floors are stained in a rich high-gloss chocolate brown. A magnificent painted white staircase beckons you upstairs. Off to the right is the formal living room, which is broken up into several intimate seating areas with two back-to-back gray velvet sofas, sculptural coffee tables, and sleek seating. The glam formal dining room would look right

at home at a hip hotel, with its urban chic rectangular table and the high-backed cream upholstered chairs by French design super-star Christian Liagre. It makes me wonder, How is it possible to have such pristine rooms with a houseful of kids and their many friends? "It's a challenge." David chuckles. "I just had a conversation with them today about keeping everything neat and they were like, 'Geez, Dad, would you lighten up a bit?'"

Happily for David, the kids prefer to hang out in the theater room downstairs that's outfitted with a giant overstuffed sectional sofa, a movie screen, and Xbox 360, as well as the luxe kitchen upstairs that boasts an adjoining sunroom with a comfy cream sofa surrounded by windows. The ultra-cool kitchen pairs stainless steel appliances, dark-chocolate-stained cabinets, and thick white Carrera marble countertops for a dramatic effect. A nine-foot-wide island with wings on both ends provides room for congregating on all three sides. It's where most of the family's meals take place and the heart of the household.

David's dream house, with its incredible views and gorgeous design, has brought an unexpected benefit to his life: he's been inspired to live in a more environmentally friendly way. He now drives less, often walking to his job, only one mile away, and he patron-izes shops and restaurants he can stroll to. Not content to have just a green renovation, he's looking into alternative sources of energy, including a wind turbine in the yard and solar panels on the roof. "Everyone has a lot of awareness now," says David. "But I want to be ahead of the rest of the universe in terms of how I live my life."

The low wainscoting in the dining room and the tall
baseboard moldings help visually to lift the height of
the ceiling. French doors lead to the backyard.

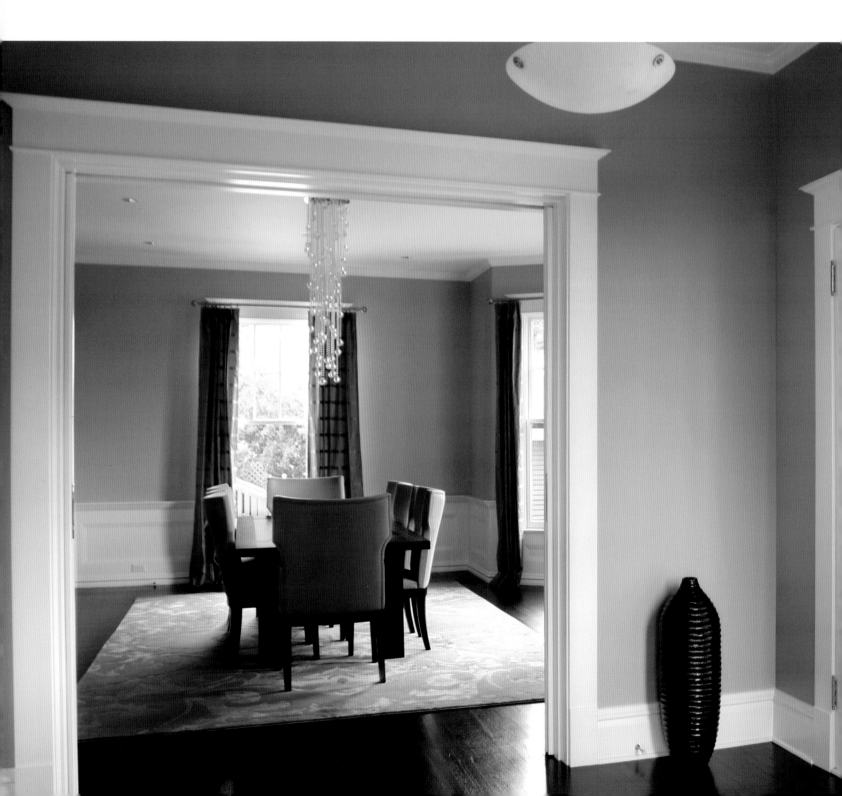

The texture of the natural wood console tabletop has movement that evokes waves of water. Similarly, the chandelier over the dining room table (see opposite) is reminiscent of water droplets, which works well with the theme.

Right: Across from his-and-her sinks in the master bath is a raised tub whose bathers can view the skyline.

Below: The master bathroom opens onto a terrace that sits atop the highest point in Seattle.

1. **SAVED ORIGINAL VEGETATION**
During construction several small plants and trees were removed, safeguarded in a greenhouse, and then replanted when the house was complete. Plywood was placed on the lawn to protect it during construction.

2. **NO CONSTRUCTION WASTE WAS BURIED**
A common practice for builders is to dump scraps into the ground and cover them with dirt or burn them. Instead, all scrap materials from the job that could be reused were recycled.

3. **SALVAGED APPLIANCES AND RECYCLABLE MATERIALS**
Old sinks, hardware, and appliances went to a grateful architectural salvage yard.

4. **WASTE MATERIALS DISPOSAL**
Oil and antifreeze from construction vehicles went to an oil disposal facility rather than a landfill, which often happens after a large job.

5. **NO ZINC PRODUCTS**
Zinc, commonly used for drainpipes and gutters, gets washed off and pollutes the groundwater. Seattle is trying to protect salmon and other marine life, so they are requiring residents to eliminate products that contain zinc.

6. **UPDATED WINDOWS**
Old leaky windows were replaced with double-paned windows that are more energy efficient.

7. **ADDED NEW WINDOWS**
To add cross-ventilation and optimize air quality, the house got additional windows in most rooms.

8. **BIODEGRADABLE CLEANERS**
During construction, only vinegar mixed with water was used as a safe, biodegradable, totally natural cleaner.

9. **DOORMAT AND SHOE RACKS AT ENTRY**
Because shoes track in a plethora of pollutants, the architects always add shoe racks and a doormat at the front and back doors, an easy way to stop bacteria and viruses in their tracks.

10. **LONG-LIFE MATERIALS**
So as not to produce waste after only a few years, the house uses long-lasting durable materials that won't have to be replaced for decades, such as a forty-year roof and marble countertops.

Right: The wood table is painted to mimic an African wood.

Far right: The extraordinary glass chandelier is a glamorous foil for the dining room table.

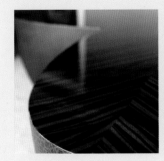

PARADISE BY THE SEA

Talib House
Fort Lauderdale, Florida

WITH THE CANALS IN FRONT AND THE SMALL POND IN BACK, IT DOES INDEED
FEEL AS IF WE ARE ON A BOAT ABOUT TO SET SAIL.
— Kaizer Talib

Drop by Kaizer Talib's stunning Fort Lauderdale home on any weekend and you're bound to find the architect and his adorably precocious six-year old daughter, Sabrina, enjoying the little Eden that Kaizer has created for them. "We swim every day," says Kaizer as we sit by the sleek pool in front of the glamorous two-story house he designed. "Of course, I try to do laps but Sabrina just wants to play so I do laps on the days she's not here," Kaizer adds, laughing, as Sabrina practices her diving skills.

When they're not taking a dip, Sabrina and Kaizer spend their days together fishing from the dock, playing boccie, or swinging from the rope swing. They pick flowers together or snack on mangoes and bananas from the twelve fruit trees they planted in front of the house. "It's like a little jungle in the front," Kaizer says. Sabrina's already well aware of the benefits of having an architect for a father; she's recently set her sights on her own green home—a magical tree house to be hidden among the branches of the giant rubber tree that sits on the front lawn. Kaizer is already drawing up the plans.

Kaizer, who was once a protégé of legendary architect Louis Kahn, initially arrived in Fort Lauderdale for a two-week vacation with his elder daughter, Natasha. It was only supposed to be a brief rest before he took a teaching job at a university in Philadelphia. But in those two weeks, he was so enticed by the vibrant Florida culture that he canceled his contract in Philadelphia and put down roots in the Sunshine State. His daughter Natasha was also smitten with the region and she's now a partner at a Miami law firm. For Kaizer, who was born in Bombay, the tropical rhythms of life in south Florida suit him perfectly. "Bombay and Miami have exactly the same weather, except Bombay has a three-month monsoon season." It was the beginning of an eighteen-year love affair with the region that's inspired by seaside living and an alluring community.

His latest house pays tribute to life on the water, taking yacht design as its inspiration. "I was tired of building the Mediterranean-style homes that are so popular here," he admits. "For my own house I wanted to go in a totally different direction." The all-white exterior mimics the yachts that pass by the house daily. To enter the home, you have to walk over an upward sloping bay bridge that crosses over a small pond, giving the effect of boarding a ship. From there you enter into a circular double height living room shaped like a ship's hull. A sleek curved staircase like those seen on cruise ships leads you up to the three bedrooms, all of which have outdoor decks for taking in the view of the network of canals in this part of Fort Lauderdale. "Did you know that we have more linear miles of canals than Venice?" asks Kaiser as we check out the balcony off Sabrina's bedroom. With the canals in front and the small pond in back, it does indeed feel as if we are on a boat about to set sail.

To break up the primarily white interior, Kaiser added bright bursts of color along at least one wall in almost every room. A dusty blue defines the kitchen, a soft red enlivens a corner of the living area, and a blue-green the color of the water frames Kasier's bed. In some cases, as in the master bath, he playfully paired two distinct colors in the same space. "I chose primary colors for Sabrina," explains Kaiser. "It also gives the house some warmth."

Designwise he kept it simple. "I like a more minimalist look," he says. He chose primarily Scandinavian and Italian furniture, drawn to their geometric silhouettes and understated colors. The most dramatic piece is a navy circular leather sofa that fits perfectly in the living area's hull-shaped living space. When

Natural materials, such as limestone, slate, granite, and maple, were chosen throughout the house to obtain harmony with nature.

The house, which sits alongside Fort Lauderdale's Intracoastal Waterway, boasts workout spaces and a saltwater infinity pool.

we point out that there are no window treatments anywhere in the house, Kaizer explains that "the views are too beautiful to cover up." He selected natural materials throughout—limestone floors in the living area, slate in the dining room, and granite for the kitchen counters. "I didn't want artificially made materials," says Kaizer. "I wanted natural stones that are durable long-term choices." Part of the appeal was also that natural materials don't contain harmful chemicals. In the kitchen he chose pressed-wood cabinets that are formaldehyde free, as are the engineered maple floors in the bedrooms that come from a sustainable-growth forest.

Because healthy living is important to him, Kaizer designed the house also to be a spa and sanctuary, with a Jacuzzi, sauna, steam room, gym, and pool. He does yoga outdoors with an instructor and meditates on the deck off of his bedroom so there is no need to commute to a gym. "I'm intrigued with the concept of the house as a health spa," explains Kaizer.

An extension of healthy living, the home is extremely energy efficient. His interest in green architecture started in the 1970s during the oil embargo, although he thought at the time that it was the beginning of a whole new way of thinking for everyone. "But as soon as the embargo was over everyone forgot about solar energy," he laments. Kaizer feels passionately that to make a house completely sustainable, you have to use a variety of methods. His goal is to have the house produce all its energy in the next couple of years when he adds photovoltaic panels on the roof for electricity, and hopefully is able to use wind-generated power. Right now, a solar hot water heater on the roof provides all the hot water needs of the house.

"I think many architects and builders forget that by using the correct orientation and taking advantage of local climate and landscape, one can easily reduce the energy impact of a building by thirty percent," he says. For Kaizer that meant using passive solar energy, orienting the house on a north-south axis with limited exposure from the south and southwest, where the impact of the Florida sun is the greatest. The majority of the windows are on the east side for the morning sun and maximum daylight, so no lights are needed during the day. The balconies have an added bonus beyond just taking in the scenery; they also provide shade and protect the rooms from getting too much heat. Having an all-white exterior, white ceramic tiles on the flat part of the roof, and radiant barrier insulation under the roof all help reflect the solar heat gain, minimizing the need for air-conditioning. Carefully placed windows are ready to catch the breezes off the water to keep the house cool.

Kaizer's initial plans to put in a wind generator to power about 20 percent of his home's energy use were stalled when he didn't get the variance he needed. "They didn't want a wind generator in an expensive living area," he says. His neighbors' arguments against the 65-foot structure were varied: "One woman worried the windmill would fall on her head; another thought it would hurt the birds." He laughs at notions he believes are preposterous. "In this country we are so backwards about alternative sources of energy." But he's optimistic about the future, and he thinks the tide is turning. "Now, because gas prices are up, I think people are more interested in renewable sources of energy," he says, adding hopefully, "I think we're ready."

Left: The kitchen cabinets are covered with a maple wood veneer, which is constructed using thermofoil, a heat process that adheres veneer to the wood backing. The porthole-like windows at the top of the dark kitchen wall bring brightness to the deep blue space.

Below: The architect-homeowner playfully painted one wall in each room with an intense primary color. In the kitchen and dining areas, the dramatic barrel-vaulted ceilings make the room seem longer and add drama to the space.

Previous pages: The daughter of the house swings on a rope attached to a giant rubber tree in the front yard.

Following page: The living room in this nautical-style home is shaped like the bow of a boat, taking visual cues from outside elements, such as the canal, the pool, and the pleasure boats that are moored on the adjacent waterway. Even the built-in shelves resemble the rungs of a ship's ladder. The shelving houses the fireplace and a flat-screen television above.

1. **SOLAR HOT WATER HEATER**
   Located on the roof, the system provides all the hot water for the house.

2. **SOYBEAN INSULATION**
   Chemical-free organic poured soybean material provides airtight insulation.

3. **PASSIVE SOLAR**
   The house is oriented on a north-south axis to limit the exposure from the south and southwest, where the impact of the sun is greatest.

4. **DAYLIGHTING**
   Most of the windows are located on the east side to provide lots of morning sun. Deep porches and balconies protect the rooms from getting too hot.

5. **SUSTAINABLY HARVESTED WOOD**
   FSC-engineered maple floors are sustainably harvested.

6. **MINIMAL WOOD USED IN CONSTRUCTION**
   By using concrete slabs on the second floor and the roof terrace, the need for wood in construction is minimized.

7. **WHITE CERAMIC TILES**
   On the flat part of the roof, the tiles reflect the solar energy away from the house, and a canvas canopy provides additional shading.

8. **METALLIC ROOFS**
   On the sloping roofs, metal reflects the sun, reducing heat gain. In Florida the government provides a $4,000 rebate for installing metallic roofs.

9. **RADIANT BARRIER INSULATION**
   Insulation installed underneath the roof also reduces solar impact.

10. **ENERGY STAR–RATED APPLIANCES**
    Energy Star–rated appliances save energy and water consumption.

Left: The master shower is fully equipped with steam for the complete spa experience. The house also has a sauna. The slatted natural wood bench is a great addition to a steam shower.

Above: The spiral stairway leading to the metal roof is painted white to reflect the sun.

SIDE BY SIDE

Moore-Breedlove and
Anderson-Boyd Duplexes
Austin, Texas

SUSTAINABLE DEVELOPMENT REQUIRES MORE DENSITY IN EXISTING NEIGHBORHOODS. THIS
PROJECT ATTEMPTS TO PUT TWO FAMILIES WHERE ONE FAMILY ORIGINALLY LIVED WHILE
STILL MAINTAINING PRIVACY AND OPEN OUTDOOR YARDS.

— Project Architect Travis Young

Previous pages, left: The stair treads are fashioned from recycled wood chips, which are strong, easy to maintain, and visually interesting, as they contain many different hues of wood tones.

Previous pages, right: The architect's main goal in conceiving this two-family duplex was to design spaces that maintained a high degree of privacy even though the spaces are literally side by side, separated only by a car port, which serves as the divider.

Opposite: The dramatic vertical window lets in a tremendous amount of sunlight, and the roof overhangs and metal sunscreens outside keep the space cool. The polished concrete floor bounces tthe light throughout the space.

Above: The interface FLOR carpet tiles beneath the coffee table are the perfect choice for minimalist design as they lie perfectly flat in the space and can be arranged in simple patterns.

When writer Emily Breedlove moved from New Jersey to Austin, Texas, she quickly set out to get to know her new town. Between writing assignments, Emily spent hours hoofing it through the hip city's varied neighborhoods. It was on one of those adventures that she came across an unusual two-story wood-paneled house that intrigued her. She was drawn to the motelesque design that featured a long rectangular silhouette, deep roof overhangs, ribbon windows, and a concrete turret. It instantly became her favorite house in town. "I loved that it was completely different than the other boring boxy houses around it," explains Emily.

A year or so later, when she and her boyfriend Roy Moore were looking to buy their own place, they met with Metro House, a local developer known for teaming up with various architects to build distinctive houses with modernist design influences. Because the 1940s tract houses that pepper the area lack the up-to-date features Roy was looking for,

such as excellent insulation and energy-efficient windows, the duo loved the idea of buying new. The developer offered to let them customize their unit by choosing from an array of flooring, cabinet, and tile options in the kitchens and baths so the house would feel like theirs. Emily checked out blueprints for a duplex unit on Justin Street and saw that the architect Travis Young had also designed her favorite local building. That little bit of kismet, paired with an alluring contemporary design, inspired the couple to take the plunge and buy the three-bedroom duplex.

Meanwhile, Robyn Anderson and Andrew Boyd were also looking for a new home. They'd become frustrated with the choppy layouts and tiny rooms of the neighborhood tract houses. Hoping new might be the way to go, they looked at the Justin Street duplex, now almost completed. Noting the open, loftlike design with a flexible floor plan and floor-to-ceiling windows that opened onto a private backyard, they were sold.

Unlike most developers, who take the easy route with cookie-cutter developments, Metro House hired Travis to design homes people would want to preserve. "They were really interested in creating a community," says Travis, who was impressed with their level of attention to the lifestyle details of their clients. But it was Travis who encouraged them to make every one of his site-specific designs green. "I still remember waiting in line to get gas with my parents during the 1970s," Travis says. "It was the source of much fear and stress." That memory looms large over all his projects, so he tries to minimize energy consumption with every design. He's also thought about how each house adds to the community as a whole. With a farmer's market, a grocery store, and a handful of restaurants cropping up nearby, he's hoping the people who live in this neighborhood will start relying on their cars less and walking or biking more.

For the Justin Street project, Travis was intrigued by the problem of maximizing a lot previously occupied by a single-family 1940s tract house. The house was moved to another location and reused, and Travis designed a two-family duplex in its place. One major design goal was to maintain privacy, making sure that each unit felt like its own individual house. He achieved that with a clever S-shaped plan with a house at either end. At the center are adjoining carports. Because the building's only shared wall is between the cars, there are never the noise complaints that usually plague residents of duplexes. Travis also kept the entrances separate. Each couple can park their cars and walk straight into their house without having to venture into each other's front yard. Each unit boasts its own backyard, and the high windows in the upstairs bedrooms provide views of the treetops, not each

other's gardens. Private breezeways with fans provide each couple with a shady outdoor retreat. It's the perfect situation for everyone. "We only see each other when we want to," says Roy, laughing.

Daylighting was another determining factor in the neomodern design. The trick was accessing as much sunlight as possible while limiting the solar heat gain from the unbearably hot Texas sun. Deep horizontal roof overhangs provide shade, working hardest in the summer, when the sun is highest in the sky. And the two-story outdoor aluminum sunscreen flanking a vertical row of windows ingeniously reflects light into the room without the heat of direct sun. Another clever touch is an elevated windowed core that rises above each roofline and floods the interior with sunlight. "One of the first things everyone notices is how much light we get," says Andrew. The roof overhangs, combined with the metal sunscreen, keep the house fairly cool, limiting the need for air-conditioning.

Because the units were built on spec, Travis created an understated interior that would work as a backdrop for each family's own style. "I wanted it to be like a gallery space," he explains. "The design would become a background for their own things." The first level of both duplexes features a minimal setting of polished concrete floors and floor-to-ceiling windows that frame a backyard view. A kitchen along the back wall opens up to a living-dining space. A contemporary staircase that pairs metal with recycled wood-chip stair treads leads to two bedrooms upstairs. But because the developers let both couples choose a number of details, including the style of IKEA kitchen cabinets, upstairs flooring, and bathroom tiles, both units have their own vibe. "Because we got to choose so

Above: The accent color is red hot in this space, inspired by the mosaic tile backsplash in the open kitchen.

Right: A glass corner allows abundant sunshine to enter the space, cutting down the need for lighting as well as bringing the outdoors into the room.

Glass panels on the stair railings
contribute to the truly airy feel of this
duplex, and the colorful abstract canvas
adds a splash of color and a visual
focal point.

many features, it really feels like it's our house," says Emily, whose kitchen has more of a pop art flair, while Andrew and Robyn's is more minimalist.

Emily and Roy relied on a black, gray, and red color scheme throughout their home that takes its cues from the kitchen's mosaic tile backsplash. Jetsons-style red plastic and metal stools lighten up the mood. A red circular wool carpet, red glass pendant lights above the kitchen island, and red striped throw pillows add some punch to the otherwise neutral space. A square wood table forms a nice textural contrast against black leather Parsons chairs in the dining area. Comfort was the inspiration for the living space, and plush overstuffed sofas and chairs are favorite lounging spots for Emily and Roy. In the master bedroom and bath, the couple dreamed of an Asian-inspired aesthetic. The graphic simplicity of a curved slatted wood headboard, tall sliding maple screens, and the pebbled stone band in the shower all exude an Eastern influence. But their favorite piece was the Chinese-style cinnabar red vanity cabinet they commissioned from local artisan Mike Keener. "We love the simplicity of Asian design," says Emily.

In Andrew and Robyn's place, gray is the primary shade, giving the overall aesthetic a more serene feeling. A boxy gray microsuede sofa and chair echo the polished concrete floors, making the large pieces almost recede into the background. FLOR carpet tiles in three shades of gray add a bit of graphic pattern to the space. To distinguish the dining area, the couple used red 1950s vinyl chairs and a matching table they nabbed at a garage

sale. The flexible space works well for the board-game and movie nights that Andrew and Robyn host every few weeks for a handful of close friends. In the kitchen, handmade cherry stools pop against white high-gloss IKEA cabinets. (The pair, who met at a local comic book convention, are major collectors of vintage comics. When they realized their kitchen drawers were a perfect size for storing comics, they ordered more cabinets and put them in Andrew's home office.)

Upstairs Andrew and Robyn chose bamboo floors. "They're hard, cheap, and renewable so they were a really appealing option," explains Robyn. Their bedroom is spacious and simple with muted colors and minimal furniture. The second bedroom is now Robyn's studio, where she paints vibrant abstracts and designs T-shirts and bags for her Web-based business.

Both couples admit that sustainable design wasn't first on their list of features they were looking for in a home, but living in an earth-friendly space has been inspiring—and healthy for their bottom line. Roy and Emily estimate their energy bills are the same for houses that are half the size of their 1,800-square-foot duplex. "I've always been into recycling and saving energy," explains Emily. "It's nice to live in a house that fits into that lifestyle."

For Robyn and Andrew, living in a green house has changed their everyday life. Although it costs a few dollars more every month, they've chosen wind power as their energy source through the local utility company. They're also bringing canvas bags to the store and walking more. "I think it's all about small changes," muses Andrew.

Below left: A one-of-a-kind cinnabar vanity cabinet, which was made by a local artisan, mirrors the Eastern aesthetic in the bathroom.

Below right: Vertical overhangs such as this one keep the hot Texas sun from overheating the space while still allowing the view to be the focus from the porch.

GREEN FEATURES

1. REUSING AN OLD HOUSE
   The developers wanted to build new and not remodel, but the 1940s tract house that stood on the lot was moved to another location in the neighborhood and bought by a family.

2. RECLAIMED LUMBER
   Beams that feature recycled wood were used for framing the house.

3. LOW-E WINDOW COATING
   The invisible film coating on windows prevents UV rays and heat from entering the house.

4. RAINWATER IRRIGATION
   The gutters and drain spouts are directed to the landscaping, cutting down on the need for additional water.

5. ABUNDANT DAYLIGHTING
   Maximizing the light in the core of the house limits the need for electric lighting during the day.

6. HEAT RECOVERY SYSTEM
   Heat generated by the air-conditioner also heats the water.

7. STAIR TREADS
   Parallam treads are made from compressed wood chips.

8. LOW-FLUSH TOILETS AND LOW-FLOW SHOWERHEADS
   Cuts down on water use by as much as 50 percent.

9. ENERGY STAR APPLIANCES
   Use less energy than their predecessors.

10. CONCRETE FLOORS
    Concrete serves as subfloor and floor surface, which saves money and resources. A non-VOC wax gives the floor its polished sheen.

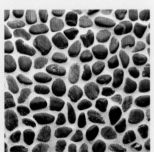

Above left: Windows are low-E coated, which keeps out harmful sun rays.

Above right: A pebblestone band was used in the bathroom for a natural effect.

Left: Parallam stair treads are straighter than wood planks, due to the composition of the material.

SUBURBAN

SIMPLY MODERN

Bennett Family Residence
Easton, Massachusetts

I THOUGHT IT WAS REALLY INCREDIBLE HOW INVESTED THEY WERE IN THE
ENVIRONMENT. IT FELT LIKE A GIFT TO DO A HOUSE FOR THEM.

—Project Architect Mary Ann Thompson

The energy-efficient windows do
not require treatments because the
home is naturally shaded by the
woods. The lack of curtains and
carpets prevents dust from
accumulating. The coffee table,
purchased online, was fashioned
from an old ship's hatch.

Previous pages, left: The chandelier above the dining room table is made from recycled aluminum shaped like the branches of a tree, which is a recurring design theme in this little house in the big woods.

Previous pages, right: This nocturnal view of the home emphasizes the sloped roof designed to minimize the summer sun.

Yes, the Bennett family dries all of their laundry on a frontyard clothesline, cooks many of their vegan meals in a solar oven, and grows their own organic produce—but, according to mom Kyla Bennett, an environmental lawyer, they don't really perceive those actions as anything special. "Everyone always asks if our dryer is broken," she says with a laugh. "But living this way is just so normal for us. It's hard even to think of what we do as different." The truth is, these model green citizens not only live in a gorgeous sustainable home but are completely committed to making every aspect of their lives as low-impact as possible. "We feel so strongly that this is the right thing to do," says Kyla.

Everyone in the family, from Kyla's husband, Don, a biostatistician, to their children, Denali, thirteen, and Eames, sixteen, makes dozens of choices each day to take as little from the earth as possible. To reduce their reliance on their car, Kyla clocks in from home, while Don, barring a snowstorm, bikes to the train station. Denali and Eames help tend the fruit and vegetable garden, which yields organic tomatoes, broccoli, blueberries, and apples (to name just a few). Staples like eggs, cheese, and milk are picked up at a nearby organic dairy farm. For summer vacations, the Bennetts get even closer to nature at their 60-acre, totally off-the-grid cabin in Vermont.

Don and Kyla met in grad school, where they were earning PhDs in ecology. Their studies only increased their green conviction. "We really understood the importance of living lightly on the earth," explains Kyla. That knowledge fueled the dream of one day building their own sustainable home. For decades Kyla kept a file of article clippings about green design. Beyond the appeal of energy savings and using recycled materials

was a more personal motivation: Eames has allergies that Kyla attributes to environmental toxins. "We wanted to build a house that was not only as green as possible but as healthy as possible," she states.

To make their eco vision a reality, they turned to Boston-based architect Mary Ann Thompson, known for her large-scale sustainable buildings and stunning designs. When the Bennetts found a densely wooded five-acre property in North Easton, they hoped Thompson would design a house for them. Since the project and the budget were small, the couple had their doubts whether Mary Ann would take them on as clients, but she instantly agreed. "I thought it was really incredible how invested they were in the environment," Mary Ann says. "It felt like a gift to do a house for them." The result of their collaboration is a 3,400-square-foot two-story rectangular house that is beautiful in its simplicity and total commitment to green living.

Inside, the house is spare and clutter-free, decorated in neutral shades of beige with an occasional splash of color in a coverlet or chairs. The understated design draws the eye toward the idyllic outdoor views. Unobstructed by curtains, the windows become canvases with New England's four seasons on lush display in the woods outside. Window treatments and rugs harbor dust and bacteria that often contribute to allergies, so the Bennetts left them out of the interior design. Kyla adds, "Our driveway is nine hundred feet long, so privacy isn't an issue."

The first floor's airy floor plan features living and dining areas and a kitchen all in one large space. When Denali practices drums, Eames plays the piano, or Don wants to jam on his bass, they block off a music area from the rest of the space with an accordion sound-muffling screen. For dinner, the family gathers at a dining table and benches handcrafted from reclaimed ash wood, lit by an ethereal recycled aluminum branch chandelier. When guests come over they often note the countertops, thinking they've caught the family in a rare ungreen moment. "They say, 'Oh, you used granite; that's not great for the environment' and I say, 'Look closer,'" says Kyla. The counters are made from Alkemi, a recycled composite material made of primarily post-industrial scrap aluminum.

The set of three Togo Ultrasuede foam sofas from Ligne Roset, like most of the furniture throughout the house, was recycled from their previous home. The iconic 1970s sofas are incredibly light and can be moved easily when Denali and Eames want to watch a movie or need more room for a jam session. Kyla and Don rounded out the interior with vintage or repurposed items, such as the industrial-chic coffee table they made from an old ship's hatch found on Craigslist. Ever the recycler, Kyla even gave a dead cedar on their property new life as a sculpture in the corner of the living area; it doubles as an eco-friendly Christmas tree.

At the top of the FSC-certified maple stairs are three bedrooms whose minimal furnishings and renewable Lyptus-wood floors continue the visual tranquility. The Zen feeling that Kyla and Don were aiming for throughout is especially evident in the master bathroom, which features a shower floor made of pebbles, and a striking Japanese soaking tub.

Building their dream home was definitely worth the effort, but it wasn't always an easy process. "The price was prohibitive for a lot of things," explains Kyla, who wishes she could have afforded to install more solar panels, nicer cabinets, and a rainwater collection system. "If I had all the money in the world our house would be platinum LEED certified, not just silver certified." In fact, even the U.S. Green Building Council's LEED certification, which measures how sustainable building choices are, from water usage to the amount of construction waste, costs a whopping $1,400. "I asked them what we would get in return for the registration fee," Kyla says. The answer? "Bragging rights." But the Bennetts made room in their budget to be a part of the LEED program, knowing that it would inspire others to build green, too.

But tight finances were a welcome challenge for Mary Ann, who was excited at the prospect of building a sustainable house for the same cost as a conventional one—a goal she achieved. While some green choices did cost more, such as creating walls from clay instead of plaster, installing recycled rubber roofing that mimics the look of slate, or choosing the nontoxic spray-in insulation, Mary Ann also steered them toward several less pricey eco options. The concrete floors on the first level provided a huge savings because the complete subfloor also serves as flooring, so there was no additional cost of putting in, say, wood floors. To soften the look, they chose a warm concrete stain that resembles worn nutty brown leather.

The couple was also clever about finding less pricey green alternatives. Don had his heart set on a cork mosaic for the laundry room floor, but the price was a prohibitive $15 per square foot. Online at Home Depot, however, they found sheets of cork for only $2 per square foot. Denali and Eames punched out circular cork cutouts and they used nontoxic glue to design and install their own mosaic floor. Another money saver? No air-conditioning. An angled roof designed to keep

The floors in the bedrooms
are made of sustainable Lyptus,
which shows fewer heel marks
than bamboo.

Above left: The floor, made of both maple and Lyptus, provides an interesting contrast in the home's design.

Above right: The light-wood bathroom vanity with the hot teal accent on the mirror and cabinet pulls softens the stonelike feel of the shower stall tiles.

Left: The strong horizontal picture window contrasts with the vertical views of the trees outside, creating a restful visual landscape and also allowing for great views of the night sky from the bed.

summer sun out, well-thought-out windows for cross-ventilation, and ceiling fans that consume half the energy of their standard cousins all keep the house cool.

Thompson facilitated savings by orienting the house to take advantage of passive solar energy, facing it south and choosing a rectangular shape that heats efficiently. The low winter sun comes in through the first level's floor-to-ceiling windows and is absorbed by the concrete floor. Additional warmth is provided by radiant heating that utilizes hot water, which travels through tubing underneath the floor. When temps are in the single digits, the Bennetts light up the two stoves that burn recycled sawdust pellets. "It's the cleanest fuel besides solar," Kyla explains. For backup on frigid nights, the upstairs bedrooms are equipped with heaters. Even so, their highest gas bill is about $120, while their neighbors spend several times that.

Throughout the entire design process, Kyla spent hours researching suppliers, materials, and green building practices. She was eager to try out the cleanest, healthiest, most sustainable materials, and excited to learn about using clay walls, which are completely nontoxic, mold resistant, and can be naturally tinted instead of painted. Because none of the local contractors had worked with clay before (it's more prevalent in the Southwest), they gave insanely high estimates to do the job. Undaunted, the Bennetts decided to do it themselves. While they were up for the challenge, they weren't prepared to spend *four months* on the job. Thanks to a family friend who is a plasterer, along with hundreds of hours on the phone with the manufacturer's support line, they got through it, although, admittedly, mistakes were made. "At first we put it on too thick, and then we didn't put in the corners correctly, but by the time we finished we were experts," says Kyla.

Going completely green was more labor-intensive than the Bennetts ever expected, but all that work paid off almost immediately for Eames. After only a few months, "not only are his allergies gone but we have fewer respiratory viruses, too," Kyla says. Although the experience of building a new green house was a challenging one, the Bennetts wouldn't change a thing. "It was exhausting and anxiety-provoking," admits Kyla about all the research, money, time, and hands-on work it took to get the house finished. But she's quick to add, "I would do it all again. I love our house."

The reclaimed-ash dining table and benches rest on the radiant-heated concrete floor, which feels delightful to walk on even during cold Massachusetts winters.

1. **PASSIVE SOLAR**
   The house faces south with a wall of floor-to-ceiling windows along the first floor to let the low winter sun in. The asymmetrical roof overhang blocks out summer sun. The rectangular shape of the house retains heat most efficiently.

2. **PHOTOVOLTAIC PANELS**
   Located on the roof, PV panels provide most of the electricity for the house. The panels are hooked up to the local utility company, which kicks in additional power when needed and buys any excess power that they produce.

3. **RECYCLED RUBBER ROOF**
   Made to look like slate, the EcoStar roof is made from recycled rubber and has a fifty-year warranty.

4. **NATURAL VENTILATION**
   Well-placed windows encourage cross-ventilation. Ceiling fans, with blades designed by an aeronautical engineer to consume half the energy of standard ceiling fans, circulate air and keep it cool.

5. **PELLET WOOD STOVE**
   With no forced air heat in the house, a pellet wood stove provides heat during cold New England winters. Burning recycled sawdust pellets provides the cleanest fuel other than solar.

6. **CONCRETE FLOORS**
   On the first floor the concrete floors absorb low winter sun and release the heat for several hours.

7. **LYPTUS WOOD FLOORS**
   The second floor has Lyptus wood throughout. A hybrid of the eucalyptus tree, Lyptus matures in just fourteen to sixteen years and is produced in a sustainable and environmentally responsible manner.

8. **CLAY WALLS**
   Clay walls are natural and nontoxic. They "breathe," pulling in the humidity and keeping the house cool.

9. **LED LIGHTBULBS**
   LED bulbs screw into any 120-volt light socket and work with dimmer switches, unlike many compact fluorescents. They use about one-thirtieth of the energy of a standard bulb and even 40 percent less energy than compact fluorescents, and can last up to 50,000 hours.

10. **RECYCLED–SCRAP METAL COUNTERTOPS**
    Alkemi, a recycled composite material made of primarily post-industrial scrap aluminum, is hard and durable.

Right: The recycled scrap-metal countertops mimic the look of granite.

Bottom left: The pebble floor in the master bedroom shower is a perfect nonslip natural option for a wet surface.

Bottom right: Cork floors are not only eco-friendly but also quiet sound absorbers, which makes them well suited for noisy laundry rooms.

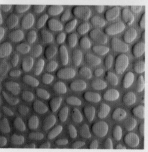

SUN HOME

McMurtrie-Service Residence
Ann Arbor, Michigan

I LOVE MY HOUSE. THE ENTIRE HOME IS LIKE A WORKING MACHINE THAT PAYS CONSTANT RESPECT TO THE SUN. LIVING HERE, I NOW UNDERSTAND OUR PLANET'S POSITION IN THE UNIVERSE.
—Genia Service

Previous pages, left: This house is specifically angled to capture the sun, with most windows facing south to maximize the available light in the room where the family spends the most time. The terrace is a great gathering spot for outdoor dining and is made of recycled plastic decking called Bear Board.

Previous pages, right: Parakeets are not native to Michigan, and this one looks like he's outside, but the bird is actually the family pet, Sun, perched indoors by the window.

Above: This connecting hallway's strong horizontal windows allow plenty of sunlight to filter into the house. The sliding cabinet doors, which hide the clutter, and the wall-mounted coat hooks are set at a child-friendly height.

Below: Beyond the small desk where mother and son work on an art project is a large pair of south-facing doors that open onto the outdoor deck.

Left: The entertainment center in the family room features movable panels made of birch veneer over plywood that is colored with aniline dye, allowing the wood grain to emerge through the color.

Although Tom McMurtrie and Genia Service adore their unconventional earth-friendly house in Ann Arbor, Michigan, initially their neighbors weren't quite as smitten. "We got an anonymous note that read 'We can't believe you built this ugly house that's going to drive down our home values,'" Genia reveals, laughing about it now. In fact, just after they moved in, two neighbors installed eight-foot fences, while another built a pagoda to block the view. Tom, who is the town's recycling coordinator, wasn't particularly worried about the negative reaction; rather, he took it as a sign that they were doing the right thing. "Tom was so calm and accepting of that fact that some people would like it and some people wouldn't," says Genia.

Soon after, they invited everyone in the neighborhood over for an open house to clear the air. Tom and Genia figured the more people knew about their eco-friendly choices, the more their neighbors would warm up to the new house. Curious neighbors ventured in along with a few fans. "One man was there right at two p.m. on the nose," Genia relates. "He said, 'I've been dying to see this house; I know it's an intelligent house.'" The party yielded plenty of positive results. "It took some people a while to get used to it," says Tom. "But once they get inside, everyone understands the green aspects and they want to learn more."

Five years ago, when Tom and Genia were envisioning their eco-modern home, they had only one requirement for the site—sunlight and plenty of it. Tom, who used to manufacture solar energy systems before his current job, had long dreamed of combining his solar and recycling know-how to build a passive solar home that utilized both recyclable and recycled materials. "Because of my job I feel

The family stays organized (and entertained) with this large natural chalkboard just off of the kitchen.

Multiple eating areas for this busy family are crucial to the very active social gatherings that take place in the Sun Home. The radiant-heat floors throughout this main living area warm the home with minimal energy because the water-filled pipes within the concrete warm the house from the floor up.

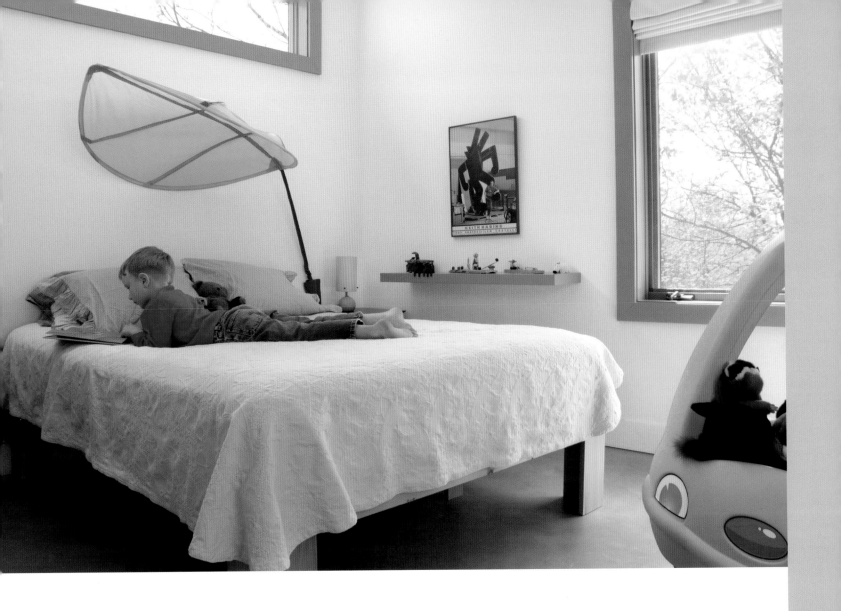

strongly about everything I do being environmentally friendly," Tom explains. So on a blustery December day when they saw the abundance of low winter sun that flooded the quarter-acre site, they knew they had found the perfect spot to build Sun Home.

In the center of the lot was an eighty-year-old magnolia that yields pink blossoms every April. "It's so incredibly beautiful," says Genia. "We knew we would build around it." The couple envisioned a house that would work as well for their son, Gary, age seven, as it would for Tom's mother, Françoise, who is in her eighties. It had to be completely wheelchair accessible with a bedroom on the first floor for Françoise plus plenty of room for Gary to play. Since they have their hands full with family, Genia wanted the feeling to be loftlike, open, and very functional with lots of hidden storage. *Low maintenance* was a term they used often.

To find an architect who knew his or her way around sustainable design, Tom cleverly sent a mass e-mail to the graduating architecture students at nearby University of Michigan. He explained his and Genia's goal of building a passive solar home and asked if anyone would be interested in designing it. A competition ensued among half a dozen architecture students. The winner was Tonino Vicari, who beat out his opposition with his in-depth knowledge of green building practices.

During the the following year, Tonino and Tom conducted precise light studies on the lot. With computer simulation, they examined where sunlight would hit different parts of the property at different parts of the day and year. They even factored in how the house would interact with the shadow lines of neighboring properties. The resulting two-story, U-shaped design frames the magnolia and features sharp angles and unexpected recesses. "The

entire geometry of the house is directly related to the sun," explains Tonino. The majority of the windows are south facing to maximize the light in the living and dining areas, and master bedroom.

"Everything inside the house is a solar collector," Tom says about the home's passive solar features. Concrete floors absorb heat in the winter when the sun is lower, and at night the heat is slowly released and radiant heat kicks in if needed. When the thermometer rises, the concrete stays cool and a north-facing whole-house fan draws out hot air. For the exterior, they chose Galvalume steel, a recycled material that has excellent thermal properties, reflecting heat away from the house in the summer and retaining heat inside the home in the winter. Tonino oriented the paneling both horizontally and vertically to create a more dynamic look. To soften all the metal, reclaimed barn siding wraps around a recess on the second floor and in the front courtyard.

Finding builders in the heart of the Midwest to bring Tonino's funky design to life wasn't an easy task, however. "Midwest builders are a very conservative lot," Tom says. "They have a certain way of doing things and that's the way they do things." The steel siding, metal roof, and concrete floors were all new concepts for the builders whom Tom interviewed, and many backed away from the job. The ones who did want to take on the project wanted to charge a small fortune to tackle so many new materials. "A framer would come in and say, 'The house has so many right angles that I have to charge you double,'" scoffs Tom.

After fifteen-months of hard work, the house was finished and Genia got to work designing the interior. The flexible space they envisioned, with open living, dining, and kitchen areas,

The vertical and horizontal metal and wood siding provide a striking contrast for the exterior of this home.

was perfect for frequent entertaining. The deck, made of 100 percent recycled plastic, lets them take their many dinner parties outside. The first floor also has a roomy bedroom and sitting room for Françoise, and upstairs houses the master bedroom, right down the hall from Gary's.

Because Genia loved the industrial airy look of the house, she wanted to keep the furnishings modern and understated so as not to compete with the architecture. All it took to furnish the place was a mix of her own pieces, like the pair of Swedish 1960s armchairs in her bedroom, plus a few of her grandmother's inspired hand-me-downs that included an organically shaped Isamu Noguchi glass-topped coffee table, and Francoise's pieces, like a 1960s Danish modern credenza. Because Tom and Genia felt strongly about not buying new pieces, the only new items were a set of four aluminum bar stools for the kitchen—because aluminum is a recyclable material—and two Todd Oldham La-Z-Boy recliners made from sustainably harvested wood.

The house fulfills the couple's wish for an incredibly functional design with an abundance of built-ins that provide more than enough storage for their busy household. Coats, boots, and outdoor gear are hidden behind the cabinets along the breezeway. A built-in along one wall of the living room hides the TV and stereo, along with books, videos, and games. Green-, yellow-, and brown-stained cabinet doors unify the look. Because birch veneer plywood is more sustainable than many hardwoods, the couple chose the same material for kitchen cabinets and an island.

Now, five years later, Tom's conviction that they would inspire others has come true. A couple down the street is interested in building their own green home and another neighbor is considering a rain barrel. The tension has faded, and they are just another home on the block, albeit a busy one. "It's party central here," says Genia. Gary's young buddies are always playing in the yard and the house is always bustling with three generations of friends. During the initial controversy over the house, one neighbor was quoted as saying, "Anyone who is willing to build around a beautiful magnolia tree can't be all bad." We wholeheartedly agree.

Above left: The recycled galvanized metal siding was chosen for its thermal properties.

Above right: The recycled plastic decking is a maintenance- and splinter-free alternative to wood.

Bottom: A neighbor made the decorative sunflowers for a flower garden that requires no watering.

1. **PASSIVE SOLAR**
   The shape of the house, the location of the windows and skylights, and the south-facing siting maximize the sunlight that comes into the house throughout the year.

2. **RECLAIMED-BARNWOOD SIDING**
   Reclaimed wood siding from two different local barns was picked up at a salvage warehouse and reused on the front of the house and a back corner on the second floor.

3. **GALVANIZED METAL SIDING**
   A recycled material and also further able to be recycled, it reflects heat away from the house in summer and retains heat in winter.

4. **RECYCLED-PLASTIC DECKING**
   The home has durable, waterproof plastic decking made from 100 percent recycled plastic.

5. **300-GALLON RAIN BARREL**
   A used rain barrel found on Craigslist collects water off the roof and sits seven feet above the ground on stilts. To water the backyard or wash their car, they simply hook up the hose and gravity starts the water flow.

6. **CELLULOSE INSULATION**
   As an alternative to conventional insulation that contains chemicals like formaldehyde, they chose insulation that was made entirely from recycled newspapers.

7. **LOW-E WINDOWS**
   Low-emittance windows are coated with an invisible film that protects against UV rays and does a better job of retaining heat in winter and deflecting the sun's rays during the summer than conventional windows.

8. **CONCRETE FLOORS**
   Concrete floors stay cool during the summer and in the winter they absorb the low winter sun and release heat for hours.

9. **RADIANT-HEAT FLOORING**
   Radiant-heat flooring is a much cleaner source of heat than forced air, which can produce dust and mold. Hot water runs through tubes underneath the floors, transferring heat to objects and individuals rather than being wasted in the air.

10. **VINTAGE FURNITURE**
    In the spirit of recycling, the house is furnished almost entirely with cool vintage furniture handed down from family or scored at local garage sales.

FROM THE ASHES

Goldberg Family Home
Seattle, Washington

OUR HOUSE WAS GREEN ON A BUDGET. WE DID AS MUCH AS WE COULD WITHIN
THAT. AS AN ARCHITECT IT WAS A GREAT EXPERIENCE TO REALLY UNDERSTAND
WHAT IT TAKES TO BUILD YOUR DESIGNS.
—David Goldberg

It's a rite of passage for an architect to design a house for himself. But Seattle-based architect David Goldberg took the ritual up a notch when he not only designed his 2,000-square-foot green house, but built it almost entirely by hand. He and his father-in-law, Adam Storch, a retired builder, and his wife, Lisa, a biochemist, spent every weekend and most evenings working on the house for almost four years, mastering everything from pouring concrete to plumbing to wiring. "We wouldn't have been able to afford this house otherwise," explains David.

The labor of love began in 1999, when Seattle's hot real estate market was reaching a full boil. The couple hoped to find a reasonably priced lot to build their own house for about $200,000 on top of the lot price, but it wasn't easy. Bidding wars and lack of affordable options were stalling their search. What they were finding wasn't that appealing. "Every time we'd find a lot it would be unbuildable—the slope was too steep or there wasn't enough space for a house and a yard," says David. To add to the stress, their real estate broker fired them after a year of not finding anything. Now David is able to laugh about it. "We took that as a bad sign."

A few months later, their new agent told them that that there was going to be an estate auction for a one-bedroom house located in the Phinney Ridge section of Seattle. The c. 1911 house, located in what had previously been a working-class neighborhood, had most likely been built for a fisherman. The lot was small, approximately one-tenth of an acre. Most recently it had been the site of a fatal fire and was completely boarded up. Although no one was allowed to step inside the smoke- and fire-damaged building, David and Lisa snuck in one evening to determine if it was

structurally sound. They pulled back one of the boards and slipped inside. "We had only about a minute to look because no one was allowed in," David recounts. It was just enough time to persuade them to make an offer. A bidding war ensued, and they weren't the highest bid. However, David had written a letter to the owners, relatives of the deceased, explaining that they were planning on keeping the house and not demolishing it to build a giant house that would be too big for the lot and neighborhood. "I think the folks in charge liked that idea," he says.

To save money, David and Lisa decided to live in the 500-square-foot house temporarily while they built their own house around it. To make the delapidated cabin inhabitable, they stripped off the interior finishes and built a small temporary kitchen that they later sold on eBay. Because the house was located far back on the lot, the plan was to build a front addition that would contain the living room, dining area, and kitchen. Then they would bunk up in the loft-living area of the front wing for a few months while they jacked up the cottage to build a three-bedroom back wing literally around the small structure. When we tour the guest room, Lisa points out one wall that has wide wood planks, the only visible sign of the old cabin. The rest is hidden behind plaster walls and ceilings. A narrow hallway, or bridge, as David refers to it, links the two wings of the house. Three small windows along the hallway are placed at David's, Lisa's, and their daughter's one-year heights. It's a lighthearted detail that reflects the Goldbergs' playful personalities.

The couple wanted their house to be small enough so they wouldn't have any wasted space and flexible enough to be a long-term home. "We didn't want to do all that work and

The upstairs living room loft features the owner's own custom-designed and -made coffee tables with clean modern lines that reinforce the calming horizontal nature of the ceiling beams, tensioned-cable handrail, and awning windows.

Above: To save money during the renovation process, the young couple lived in this loft space located in the front wing of the house.

Opposite: The hallway windows are cut into an existing wall from the original house at just the right heights for mom, dad, and daughter.

sell it to someone else," says David. With three bedrooms in the back wing and the possibility of converting the office to make a fourth, there's no need to move anytime soon. The home's I-shaped design maximizes the small lot. "We didn't want to build a rectangular box; we wanted to preserve as much outdoor space as possible," explains David. "Because the house has two wings, that creates two distinct outdoor spaces, making the lot feel larger."

They did all the framing themselves and David studied up on plumbing, wiring, and pouring concrete. Lisa did much of the finish work, painting and refinishing wood. It was, to say the least, a test of their relationship. "It was physically exhausting and it took so much longer than we thought," says David. "We definitely had our moments." For Lisa, the hardest part was living with a constant mess and never being settled in. "I don't think we ever considered giving up," admits David. "But it was much more stressful than having a baby and that's a big life transition." David estimates they did about 80 percent of the work themselves, but by the time they got to framing the back part of the house, they did hire that out. "We needed to move a little faster; we wanted to start a family," David remembers.

For David, who has been practicing sustainable design since the beginning of his career with clients like the outdoor outfitter REI, it was important that his house follow green building practices. "Our house was green on a budget," explains David. "We did as much as we could within that." They couldn't afford to put in photovoltaic panels on the roof or solar collectors to heat hot water, but the house is set up so they can in the future. However, they found that plenty of green features like bamboo and cork floors

cost less than conventional counterparts. Being on a tight budget inspired them to get creative and maximize their materials. Salvaged Douglas fir from a demolished building was used for the floors in the bridge hallway, the stair treads, and the bathroom sink countertop.

Located in a neighborhood filled with 1930s Craftsman-style homes, the house's sharp angles, tilted metal roofs, and two-structure design stand out. It's the only contemporary house on the block. But David points out that he chose cedar siding to minimize the contrast and link the house to the neighborhood's wood-sided houses. It also helps that each wing is only two stories so it doesn't dwarf neighboring homes.

The first thing I notice about the interior is how incredibly uncluttered it is—there's not a book out of place. "We're messy by nature," jokes David. "So having a place to put everything and not having too much stuff around suits us." It's also an added bonus for having an active toddler. Jillian, the couple's three-year-old, can't get into too much trouble in the clutter-free house. "There's a lot of open space for her to play in," says David. "And not a lot of stuff for her to mess with." Jillian seems to love the space, giving us her own guided tour.

For the interior design, the plan was simple: keep everything calm with minimal furniture and color. "Our lives are hectic," admits David. "So coming home to a soothing, simple space is really nice." The emphasis throughout is on natural materials, primarily wood. David and Lisa favor light-hued grains, and keeping all the wood pieces in the same pale shade gives their rooms visual continuity and an organic, Zen, Japanese teahouse vibe. White walls throughout unify the space and concentrate

the emphasis on a few well-chosen pieces. In the front wing, maple cabinets and countertops from the Home Depot, medium-density fiberboard walls, and 1960s teak Danish modern chairs and table from a nearby thrift shop add to the monochromatic scheme. In the upstairs living room loft, comfy black wool upholstered sofas and two leather Knoll chairs, a favorite of architects everywhere, surround a table handmade by Lisa. Not to be outdone by her husband, who was doing much of the heavy construction work, Lisa took a furniture class during construction and crafted the coffee table out of aluminum panels David had leftover from a job. She made a wood base to frame the geometric panels and topped them with glass. Lisa also designed and built the bed and end tables in their bedroom. How did she find the time

during all the construction? "She's very artistic and very motivated," says David. "I'm so lucky."

The couple's penchant for organic minimalism extends to Jillian's room. A simple wood crib and a white bureau that stashes toys and books are the only pieces of furniture. A bright blue area rug provides a burst of color.

For David, the whole experience gave him better insight into his work. "As an architect it was a great experience to really understand what it takes to build your designs." But even better, building a house together has made the couple's bond even stronger. "We have a really wonderful place that we wouldn't have had otherwise; it's something we're both really proud of," he says. "We've both accomplished a lot on our own, and it was incredible to do this together."

Above left: In Jillian's room, the ladder leads straight to her favorite place—the play loft—where she spends most of her quiet time reading or imagining it as her castle.

Above right: Jillian can easily explore the spaces intentionally designed to be open, clutter-free, and child-friendly.

Right: The exposed piping below the sink requires less wood than an enclosed cabinet would, making it a great option for people who like industrial style and are seeking to cut costs where they can.

Below: Despite the all-consuming renovation process, Lisa found time to design and build their light-hued wooden master bed and end tables, all of which echo the pale shades found throughout the rest of the home.

Above: A sunny spot on the outdoor deck reveals the two different-toned woods that make up the paneled area connecting the two wings of the house (right side of photograph).

Right: Due to the family's limited yard space, they created an organic garden in giant planters alongside the house.

1. **RECYCLED THE ORIGINAL HOUSE**
By literally building around the original house, they were able to save it so the materials wouldn't go into a landfill.

2. **CONCRETE/FLY ASH FOUNDATION**
Fly ash is a by-product of coal-burning power plants. In the foundation and the floors, 50 percent fly ash is mixed in with the concrete to make it stronger and more water resistant.

3. **RAIN BARREL**
An 85-gallon rain barrel in the back of the lot collects water that is then used to irrigate the drought tolerant landscaping.

4. **PLANTED TREES**
The Goldbergs planted three maples on the east side of the house and three on the south to provide partial summer shade as they mature.

5. **NO AC**
Strategically placed windows encourage excellent cross-ventilation. Ceiling fans circulate air throughout the house.

6. **RADIANT-HEAT FLOORING**
Hot water runs through pipes underneath floors when Seattle winters get frigid.

7. **SALVAGED DOUGLAS FIR**
Wood salvaged from a demolition site was used for stair treads, hallway flooring, and bathroom counter.

8. **CORK FLOORS**
All of the bedrooms have cork flooring, a softer and sustainable alternative to hardwood.

9. **LIMITED RUGS**
To keep the air quality clean, area rugs are used sparingly throughout the house.

10. **LOW-VOC FINISHES**
All paints and finishes had low levels of toxic volatile organic compounds.

Right: Cork flooring is made from byproducts of the cork-making process; cork is derived from the inner bark of the cork oak tree.

Far right: Salvaged wood from a local construction site was used to make the stairs in the house.

CLIFF DWELLERS

Skillman Family Home
San Carlos, California

I WOULD CHARACTERIZE THE DESIGN AS WARM MODERN. WE HAVE KIDS AND THEY WANT THINGS TO BE COZIER AND WARMER, SO WE MADE A POINT TO HAVE THINGS NOT LOOK STARK THE WAY SOME CONTEMPORARY HOUSES CAN.

—Laurel Skillman

Previous pages, left: The couple's expansive master bedroom boasts a view of their vanishing pool designed to look like a natural waterfall cascading down the hill.

Previous pages, right: An exterior shot of the house shows the green roof made of pebbles and desert plantings.

The one-acre hillside parcel had been sitting on California's otherwise hot real estate market for eight months when Peter and Laurel Skillman found it. "No one could figure out what to do with it," explains Peter about the steep site. But with gorgeous trees and native grasses plus a beautiful view of the canyon below, it spoke to the couple and they immediately made an offer that was quickly accepted. Later that week, however, they researched the cost of building their own house, a first for them, and found that the building permits alone would cost them more than $40,000. "I got really scared," admits Peter. They reluctantly decided to pull out of the deal.

A few months later they were still without a new home, and with two children—Kaia, now nine, and Clark, eleven—they were craving more space. "The reality when you go shopping for a house in the Bay Area is that the prices are astronomical," says Laurel, marketing director for *Dwell* magazine. "You look at a hundred houses and they're all awful. You think to yourself, I can't believe I would be spending all this money to live here." But one morning, Peter, a vice president at the Palm computer company, noticed that the hillside lot's For Sale sign was missing. He put in a call to the owner, curious as to who had bought the property. The owner explained that the land still hadn't sold, but seeing the For Sale sign every day was so depressing he finally took it down. "I was talking out loud and I said, 'Boy, if it was ten percent less I would have done it,'" revealed Peter. They had a deal.

Peter, who's had a lifelong love affair with design and architecture, spent the next few days sketching a design for the house. He envisioned a two-story house cascading down the hillside with an infinity pool below. The house would require no heating or cooling and

would rely on solar energy. He brought the sketch to architect Rod Freebairn-Smith, who "added nuance and made it wonderful." For Peter, an avid environmentalist, it was important that his design work with the land not only visually but literally as well. "So many environmentally sensitive homes are totally unattractive and not places I would want to live," he states. "I really wanted to show people that you can live in an incredibly compelling and beautiful sustainable home."

But the couple hit another snag when it came time to get bids on the design. Contractors quoted estimates that were about 50 percent more than what they could afford. It was an unwelcome surprise, and "the whole process was frightening," admits Peter. "I would wake up at four a.m. and try to figure out how we were going to manage our cash flow." Not wanting to give up, the couple put their heads together and came up with a clever, albeit labor-intensive, solution. They would hire a contractor to build the home's shell—the framing, rough plumbing, the roof, the foundation, and the exterior stucco—and they would finish the rest themselves. "We were so fired up about the house that we were totally committed to that level of involvement," explains Laurel.

One of the reasons they were able to enter so confidently into what would be a terrifyingly daunting challenge to most people is that Peter is a master do-it-yourselfer. "He sees something done once and he's like, 'I can do that,'" explains Laurel. "He has so much confidence and faith in himself, and it works." Peter did all the finish plumbing work, the lighting, the metalwork, the wiring (all 2.6 miles of it), and even designed the kitchen cabinets and some of the furniture. He wasn't afraid to get something wrong, and would

Previous pages: The industrial-chic beams are as much a style choice as a budgetary one. The splashes of primary color in the hanging fixtures and red chairs tie in to the colorful painting in this extraordinary room.

keep learning, researching, and working until he got it right. "The first time I did the electricals, the inspector came in and put everything that was wrong in broad categories," says Peter. "A week later he came back to check my work and pointed out a few specific problems. By the next week it was all correct," says Peter. Laurel was in charge of ordering everything off eBay—stockpiling sinks, fixtures, switches, faucets, bathtubs, shower fittings, even a wine fridge. The couple devoted at least twenty hours a week for two and a half years to the project. "The house was way beyond our financial means," says Peter. "But we were able to fund it by building it ourselves."

The couple wanted the house to melt into the hillside, both structurally and visually. "We didn't want just another beige stucco house," states Peter. For the exterior they color-matched a piece of the cinnamon-colored bark of the Pacific Madrone to tint the exterior stucco. Paired with aluminum linear elements, it looks from a short distance like wood siding. A sod roof with drought-resistant plants helps the flat roof blend in with the landscape.

Inside, the home is simply breathtaking, with a hip design sensibility and gorgeous views. High ceilings and lots of windows wash the upstairs open living-dining and kitchen space with light. Well-placed skylights pour sunlight through the structural metal and wood tresses that cast graphic shadows along the polished concrete floors. While the walls are primarily cream, Laurel and Peter added small blocks of reds, blues, and brown to break up certain spaces and add warmth. They chose Donald Kaufman Color for their intense pigments. Although at the time the company didn't have a low-VOC line, Laurel circumvented that by ordering Donald Kaufman tints

and added them to Benjamin Moore Ecospec non-VOC bases purchased from the local paint shop. The jolts of color throughout are in unexpected locations, the wide frame of a doorway, above the hearth, or behind the headboard in the master bedroom. "We were going for a Piet Mondrian effect," says Peter.

"I would characterize the design as warm modern," says Laurel as we tour the house. "We have kids and they want things to be cozier and warmer, so we made a point to have things not look stark the way some contemporary houses can." For this effect they chose modernist-inspired pieces with sculptural forms that don't skimp on comfort. Boxy sofas and chairs provide cushy spots for vegging with the kids. Tall red stools set up against the CaesarStone countertops in the kitchen island provide a comfortable perch for breakfast, snacks, and doing homework. Peter designed the bamboo cabinets from a computer program, with engineered stone counters selected because of their durability. "Because the kitchen is open, you're connected to the rest of the space," says Peter. "Cooking almost becomes like performing in front of everyone." In the center of the kitchen is a small island that hides the recycling center. "People don't realize how much you can recycle," says Peter. "We generate four times more recycling than trash." Much of what's left over ends up in the composting pile in back of the house.

Eames molded plywood chairs surround a dining table Peter crafted. "We kept seeing things we liked and Peter kept saying he could make a better design himself," says Laurel. Hanging glass light fixtures by Karim Rashid add character. Laurel picked them out because "they felt different; we didn't want anything typical."

A wall of windows allows the spectacular sunset to be a focal point from the bed.

Windows on one side of the house are always open to
allow for the air to flow through. Polished concrete
floors keep the décor light and airy. Sunlight absorbed
into the floors continues to warm them into the night.

A rooftop skylight allows sunshine to pour straight through this mountaintop hideaway. The graphic design casts spectacular shadows across the concrete floor and the walls.

Down the bamboo stairs are the bedrooms—the most stunning is Peter and Laurel's. Floor-to-ceiling windows take in the canyon view and the infinity pool right outside. They can take a dip in the evening, then towel off and climb into bed. For lazy mornings they've set up a café-style table and chairs for reading the paper and starting the day. Because of the views, the room needed little in terms of furnishings. A simple platform bed and side tables Peter designed completed the room. The kids' rooms are happy and colorful, with sturdy wood furniture and brightly patterned sheets.

The children are as content in their new space as their parents and intrigued by the home's green elements. "I'm pretty happy about saving so much energy," says Kaia. "I like the solar panels and I feel good that I'm not wasting a lot of energy." For Peter and Laurel it's a dream come true and well worth all the work it took to get here. "This has been the most significant expression of design in my life," says Peter. "I feel so lucky to live here."

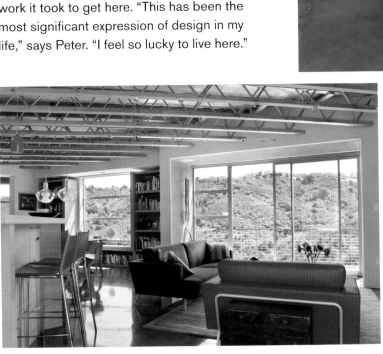

Above: Natural stone walls in the bathroom are positioned in a random color pattern, which adds intrigue to the space and, combined with the bamboo cabinets, turns this bathroom into a spa-like haven.

Left: Because of the busy open web ceiling joists, which save on material and built-in book shelves, the room works well with simple furnishings in solid colors.

1. **FLY ASH**
   A by-product of coal-burning power plants, fly ash can be mixed with concrete to make it stronger. The foundation and concrete floors contain 25 percent fly ash.

2. **ROOF OVERHANGS**
   Four-foot roof overhangs prevent summer sun and heat from entering, keeping the house cool.

3. **PHOTOVOLTAIC PANELS**
   Located on the hillside to get maximum sunlight, the 5-kilowatt system handles about 95 percent of the home's energy usage.

4. **SOLAR HOT WATER**
   Solar collectors provide all the hot water needs for the house.

5. **NO AC**
   Strategically placed windows and ceiling fans keep the house cool without air-conditioning.

6. **RADIANT-HEAT FLOORING**
   Although the house rarely needs heat due to a south-facing site that maximizes solar gain and heats up the concrete floors, radiant heat warms up when additional heat is needed.

7. **LED LIGHTS**
   Because LED lights use only 20 percent of the energy of an incandescent bulb, they're a more efficient alternative. They also don't flicker the way compact fluorescents do.

8. **BAMBOO CABINETS AND STAIR TREADS**
   Bamboo is a sustainable wood that takes only four years to reach full growth. Because it's also durable, it's a great choice for high-traffic stair treads and cabinets in a busy kitchen.

9. **SALVAGED DOORS**
   All the interior doors were salvaged from an office building being torn down nearby.

10. **SALINE POOL**
    A chemical-free alternative to chlorine, a saline pool uses salt to sterilize the pool. Another plus? Great for your skin and healing for your whole body.

Above left: The cubbyhole in this sleek armoir provides a cozy space for more green, in the form of a native California succulent.

Above right: Lighting designer Karim Rashid created this pendant fixture for the George Kovacs collection.

Bottom: Although it looks like wood, the exterior of the house is actually made of stucco with a redwood tint.

ECOMANOR

Seydel Home
Atlanta, Georgia

I WANT PEOPLE TO KNOW GREEN DESIGN DOESN'T HAVE TO LOOK LIKE A LOG CABIN.
—Laura Seydel

Growing up the daughter of CNN founder and green crusader Ted Turner was more than enough inspiration for Laura Seydel to make it her life's mission to save the planet. "He really influenced me," she says about her dad, who has a hand in wildlife and forest preservation, solar energy, and sustainable farming, to name just a few of his eco ventures. "I learned so much from him and was able to travel and really be in touch with what's going on with our planet." Today Laura is a committed environmental activist. She is the chairman of the Captain Planet Foundation, which works in partnership with the green superhero cartoon television show, and is cofounder of Mothers & Others for Clean Air, a group that raises awareness about the link between asthma and air pollution. She's also a frequent lecturer spreading the word about living green. Clearly, like her father, Laura doesn't think small. "It's been our mission to educate people about saving our planet," she explains. Married to Rutherford Seydel, a transaction and environmental lawyer, Laura's the mother of three: Vassar, twelve; John R., fifteen; and Laura Elizabeth, ten.

Having just completed building a glamorous Tudor-style green manor home in Atlanta, Laura invited us to come take a look at the house she calls EcoManor. Not content just to enjoy living in her gorgeous 6,000-square-foot house, Laura opened up the property to local environmental, school, architecture, and even gardening groups. She wants her home to serve as an educational tool to inspire builders, architects, and homeowners. "I want people to know green design doesn't have to look like a log cabin," she says. "I also want them to know it's good for your bottom line; oil is only supposed to go up in price."

Right from the early planning stages, while envisioning the house, Laura set her sights on LEED certification. "We want to lead by example," she says. The house is the first ever LEED-certified manor home and the first LEED residence in the South. "We set out to be a regional model of sustainability," says Laura. But because of the lack of environmental knowledge in the area, building a sustainable southern house had its challenges—especially because they hoped to source all of their materials and products from within a 500-mile radius. "Even at the home improvement store, they didn't know what low-VOC paint was," reveals Laura. "It was completely surprising to me that the home building industry was so late to come to healthier building."

The Seydels wanted to make sure that every single aspect of their house was sustainable, so they spent an enormous amount of time trying to research, compare, and find the best eco products. But after it took them two long months just to choose an earth-friendly toilet, Laura knew she needed help. "We thought, if this is the way it's going to be with every detail, it's going to be a ten-year project!" Enter Jillian Pritchard Cooke, an interior designer who specializes in sustainable projects. Jillian's first step was to to set up some green guidelines with Laura to keep things focused. Everything had to be energy efficient, chemical-free, and recycled or sustainable.

Jillian and Laura had an added advantage of having known each other for years (Jillian has also designed projects for Ted Turner), so Jillian knew firsthand how they live (busy) and what kind of style would work for them (upscale yet kid friendly). But making a manor home feel warm and inviting yet elegant is a tall order. Jillian began by warming up the house with an abundance of luscious colors. She devised a clever color concept, dividing the house visually into the four seasons. The downstairs living and dining rooms are influenced by the beachy colors of summer, with sunny yellow walls, blue-green curtains that mimic the sea, and soft beige upholstered sofas the color of sand. Autumn makes an appearance through the kitchen and in the rich orange walls of Laura's office, and sofas and pillows in the same bright hue jazz up the family room. Upstairs, Laura and Rutherford's roomy bedroom conveys serenity, with cool blue walls, a taupe headboard and armchairs, and rich chocolate curtains and throws—just the place for cocooning in the winter. Down the hall, the children's rooms are inspired by spring. The girls' rooms are bursting with pretty pink and soft rose floral patterns against apple green and yellow walls, while their brother's space is a happy yellowy green and reflects his dad's and his passion for the Atlanta Thrashers hockey team and his grandfather's love of the Braves!

Because the family entertains on a large scale, often hosting fund-raisers for environmental causes, the public rooms like the living and dining area are more formal. The roomy foyer, featuring a roundabout upholstered in a rich cotton velvet, is set in between the living and dining spaces so the three rooms become one large entertaining space. Plenty of seating, in the form of chairs, sofas, and even the steps, lets them entertain up to sixty guests on a regular basis. Rutherford and all three kids are avid pianists, so a grand piano passed down from Rutherford's family takes center stage in the living room and is the site of more than a few mini concerts.

It was important for Laura to incorporate as many antiques as possible in the spirit of recycling, so Jillian intertwined family heirlooms like the nineteenth-century dining table and the eighteenth-century needlepoint chairs among the design. Although the house is new, the Seydels wanted it to look like an older manor home, so nineteenth-century-inspired architectural details—such as the living room's cast stone fireplace crafted out of a composite material that only looks like real stone—add character to the space. Striking cast-iron chandeliers are modeled after French eighteenth-century designs. Large doors inspired by those found in English Tudor homes are made out of pressed wheat with an exterior veneer. "So often we think of eco-sensitive design as being granola," explains Jillian. "But this home proves you can have all the elegance you want."

Adjacent to the dining room is the library, with wood-paneled walls and antique carpets for an old-world aura. The desk is Jacobean, passed down from Laura's family. Down the hall, the kitchen is light and airy with white cabinets and white countertops. While it looks like a standard upscale kitchen, this one has cabinet boxes made of renewable pressed hay; the doors have Lyptus-wood fronts. The island countertop is made from Silestone.

Once you move into the home's private spaces, starting with the family room, the look becomes more and more modern and colorful. The family room features plenty of sofas and plush armchairs for hanging out, watching TV, and playing chess, a Seydel family passion. All of the new upholstered pieces in the house, like the two orange sofas, are crafted using sustainable wood, chemical-free fillers, and fabric made of natural materials. Covering the furniture in luxuriously comfortable fabrics was one of Laura's major requests, but it was tricky to find completely renewable and synthetic-free textiles. "The problem was we would walk into a showroom and fall in love with so many fabrics and maybe ten percent were green,"

Custom-made recycled scrap-iron chandeliers give
the brand-new home an old-world feel. The dining
table is a nineteenth-century antique, and the
needlepoint chairs are from the eighteenth century.

The old-world style of the kitchen does not prevent the use of new types of eco materials throughout, such as the concrete and recycled-glass countertops and the renewable hay cabinet interiors.

Previous pages: The living room offers plenty of seating surrounding the cast-stone gothic-inspired fireplace. The room's strong symmetry, created in part by the flanking windows and mantel ornaments, lends both balance and comfort to the home. The grand piano is a family heirloom.

Below left: The cotton bedspreads in the daughter's bedroom are made by Pine Cone Hill and designer Annie Selke, who is known for her colorful, homespun creations. The desk features a full tackboard for hanging prizewinning ribbons. The 100-percent wool carpet sits on certified wood flooring. The unique ceiling fixture from the Atlanta Furniture Mart features handcrafted glass beads.

Below: A private collection of glass animals adds color and whimsy beneath a pair of heirloom child's dresses.

Bottom: The master bathroom receives natural light from solar tubes that tunnel the sun through the roof to the ceiling.

Opposite: The antique furniture in the daughter's bedroom has been reupholstered with 100 percent natural fabrics.

Right: A touch of Americana jazzes up the corner in a room that has a sports theme for the Seydels' teenage son, John R.

Below: The bedding in the teen son's room is fashioned from bamboo. The sisal rug, by Merida, is made from hemp, jute, bamboo, and seagrass. The eight-panel wood door leading to the bathroom is veneered with Lyptus over a wheat core that is free of formaldehyde.

says Jillian. "We only wanted to use renewable resources like cotton, linen, wool, jute, and silk, nothing produced with polymer, which leaves a lingering gas, or artificial materials like rayon, viscose, or polyester." The fabrics were one of many details that Laura and Jillian refused to compromise on. They knew that with a little extra effort they could find everything they needed in earth-friendly form. "We haven't had to sacrifice anything," says Laura. "The house is really representative where luxury comes naturally."

For Laura the house was a chance to connect with her children about the power of standing behind your beliefs. "Our kids are very passionate about this," explains Laura. "They are very worried about the future of the planet and global warming." Laura's son, John R., even signed his mother up to speak at his school. "My son encouraged me to come talk because so many students don't know about what's going on with the environment, they're not even recycling," says Laura. Beyond her community and national outreach Laura wants to demonstrate that the power of change starts at home. "My kids really understand that I'm committed to this," says Laura. "I'm on twelve environmental boards and they understand that if sometimes I'm not with them it's because I'm fighting for clean water and clean air." Laura and Rutherford just may be giving her children the same gift Laura's father gave her, a belief and passion that they can help save the planet, one house, one family, and one community at a time.

Opposite: Seydel daughters Vassar and Laura Elizabeth spend time in the family's art room. This is one place where the family creates and also displays the fruit of the children's artistic endeavors. The floor is covered in Marmoleum, which is an eco-form of linoleum and soft underfoot.

Above: In a green house, what better table dressing than three pots of grass? This additional dining table off the family room moves outdoors when the Seydels want to dine al fresco under their covered porch.

Right: The desk in the library is a favorite family heirloom that has been passed down for generations. The carpet is also an antique.

Far right: The bathroom vanity is an antique made from bamboo and purchased from J. Tribbel. The lights are controlled by occupancy sensors that turn off automatically when the room is vacant.

Above: Countertops are made by Dex Studios, which mixes concrete with recycled accents to make strong visual surfaces.

Bottom: The red and white natural fabric in the guest room is proof that eco-fabrics don't have to be bland.

1. **CELLULOSE INSULATION**
   Cellulose insulation, made primarily from recycled newspapers, is highly efficient, sealing the home against air infiltration to maximize energy efficiency.

2. **MARMOLEUM FLOORS**
   Marmoleum flooring is made from natural raw materials, including linseed oil, rosins, and wood flour with a natural jute backing. It's installed with solvent-free adhesives and no VOCs.

3. **GEOTHERMAL HEATING**
   Geothermal heat pumps use the stable 51 degrees F. of the ground to provide heating and cooling to the house. In the winter, using geothermal heat reduces bills by more than 50 percent of what they would be with a propane furnace. In the summer, geothermal cooling keeps the house cool for a third less than conventional central air-conditioning systems.

4. **RAINWATER COLLECTION**
   Rainwater is collected in large cisterns and used for flushing the toilets and irrigating the landscape.

5. **GRAY WATER SYSTEM**
   Dish, shower, sink, and laundry water (gray water) is reused for watering the plants and lawn.

6. **COMPUTER-CONTROLLED ENERGY SYSTEMS**
   A touch-screen computer system controls all the major systems in the house, including entertainment, security, communications, water collection, lighting, and climate control. Energy and water usage are observable and controlled up to the minute.

7. **DOORS**
   The Humabuilt Wheatcore interior doors have cores made of rapidly renewable resources with wood veneer exteriors. They are FSC certified, use ultra-low-VOC water-based adhesives, and contain no formaldehyde.

8. **TUBULAR SKYLIGHTS**
   Solar tubes from the roof allow light to reach into interior closets and bathrooms that don't have windows. The glass used in the skylights and tubing blocks all infrared heat and fade-causing UV rays, while letting in abundant natural light.

9. **NATURAL, SUSTAINABLE FABRICS**
   Only 100 percent natural fabrics without chemical treatments were used for upholstery, bedding, and curtains. Fabrics in either cotton, silk, wool, linen, jute, and hemp were used throughout.

10. **RECYCLED-CONTENT COUNTERS**
    Eco-friendly countertops made from concrete mixed with recycled materials, including mother-of-pearl, glass, and marble, are a gorgeous and strong alternative to quarried stone.

RURAL

UP IN THE TREETOPS

Johnson-Chronister Home
Austin, Texas

I'VE ALWAYS WANTED TO LIVE IN A CASTLE. THIS IS THE NEXT BEST THING.
—Lisa Chronister

"When green architects only design contemporary houses, they really miss an opportunity to connect with more people," says Austin-based architect Elliot Johnson, lamenting the lack of eco-sensitive architectural options. Fortunately for clients who love old-world style and believe in sustainable design, Johnson creates grand European Revival residences that are both beautiful and eco friendly. "I think you can do any style you want and make it green," he says.

A gorgeous example of his philosophy is Elliot's own English Tudor–style carriage house that he shares with wife Lisa Chronister, a librarian. When you first see the charming 1,500-square-foot home with old-fashioned architectural elements, such as gabled roofs, stained glass, and arched faux-stone doorways, you feel as if you've stepped back in time. To enter the house you have to walk over a quaint bridge with cedar post railings through a pretty arched doorway featuring a stained-glass grapevine motif made by Lisa. Just down a short hallway on the second level of the antique-filled two-story home, is their dusty-green country kitchen that opens to the living room with an adjoining dining room. The bedroom is on the lower level, and both stories boast covered porches that overlook a canyon abundant with tall Spanish oaks and cedars. The eco surprise is that the house is partly constructed of cast earth, a mix of earth and gypsum that's poured into molds to form walls. "It's the most environmentally friendly form of construction because it uses no wood at all," Elliot explains. It has the added benefit of absorbing moisture, keeping the temperature cool.

Fascinated by cast earth construction for years but with no hands-on experience, Elliot gamely decided to test it out for the first time

The walls are made of cast earth, a form of construction that does not use wood but rather is a mix of earth and gypsum. The homeowners spent months creating the textured walls, using spatulas to make a swirling pattern. A newel post at the bottom of the stairs is from a Texas cedar cut from the homeowners' property; the wrought-iron handrail was crafted by a local artisan.

on his own house. But the seemingly perfect building material wasn't as easy to work with as he hoped—the decomposed granite in the mix absorbed too much moisture, causing walls to crack. But adding limestone screening, a waste material found in local limestone quarries, solved the problem. Another obstacle was getting the poured earth into the forms before it hardens, a process that takes only fifteen to ninety minutes. Because his house is located on a hilly, densely wooded five-acre lot, there are no completely flat areas, which makes operating the mixer and pump truck and forming the walls incredibly difficult. After the exhausting process of working with cast earth on the first level, Elliot decided to complete the house with stucco. But the experience didn't sour him on cast earth. "If I had a flat lot and more time, I could have completed it," he states. In fact, he's since finished building two top-to-bottom cast earth houses for clients, with positive results. "I used our house as a learning curve," says Elliot. "I think it's an amazing material."

For the interior, Elliot and Lisa understood that the design needed to be in keeping with the elegance and drama of the exterior. To give the place old-house character, the couple scoured local salvage warehouses for antique doorknobs and hardware with European flair. "We love the English and French country look," explains Elliot. "We wanted it to look like an old European carriage house." All the doors, including a nineteenth-century French pair, are salvaged. The French country–style kitchen was crafted from a mix of vintage and new cabinets, all painted the same shade of pale green. Wide-plank cypress floors throughout mimic the style of flooring that was popular two centuries ago. The couple furnished the house primarily with antiques,

Arched doorways throughout the house give it old-style European flair and accentuate the height of the ceiling. The arches were created to provide a visual separation between the rooms while still allowing in natural light. The wide-plank cyprus floors maintain the historical feel of the home.

The kitchen's "stone wall" is actually concrete designed to mimic the look of stone. Half of the cabinetry was found at a local salvage warehouse while the other half was newly constructed. The pale green paint pulls it all together. Homeowner Lisa Chronister spent five weeks creating the stained-glass grape motif on the front door.

Above: The stained-glass lamp,
rococo-style bed, antique carpets,
and damask curtains give the
bedroom an old-world ambience.

Opposite: The tile flooring
is a smart solution for homes
in climates with a lot of humidity.
The mirror, a family heirloom,
reflects the theme of arches
throughout the house.

but reproductions like the rococo-style carved
wood bed and eighteenth-century-style
tapestry chairs filled in when they couldn't find
the real thing. "We love the quaintness and
whimsy of old things," says Lisa.

Rich yellow and muted green hues that
might have graced the walls of an English
country house were chosen for their soft
backdrop and historical nod. Opulent red
damask curtains, navy-and-red-striped
wingback chairs, and fringed orange pillows
punctuate the space with more dramatic color.
The key to ensuring that the grand elements
didn't overwhelm the small space is the well-
edited design. Built-in bookshelves and
cabinets in the living room and bedroom keep
clutter in check.

Stained glass is another of the couple's
old-world passions, but when they learned
how expensive both new and old pieces were,
they decided to take a class and learn to make
stained glass themselves. After just a few
years, Lisa is a pro. When she's not working at
the local community college's library, she can
be found repairing antique transoms or
crafting new scenes. "I'm very influenced by
Tiffany stained glass," she says. "I love
landscapes and florals." All of the stained
glass in the house was done by Lisa, including
the pièce de résistance, the grand front door,
custom metal with a grape and vine motif that
took her two hundred hours to complete.

But behind all the decorative flourishes lies
a very energy-efficient eco-friendly home with
soy-based insulation, compact fluorescent
bulbs in every light fixture, and Energy Star
appliances. A black water filtration system
recycles all the water used in the house
(including sewage) for irrigating the landscape. Elliot's initial interest in sustainable
design sprang from a worry about the coun-

try's dependence on foreign oil. Elliot strongly believes that part of the solution lies in green building. "I think the future of our country depends on us changing the way we do things," he explains. But Elliot is optimistic about the future. "We're really in the infancy of green design," he states, noting a huge increase in clients coming to him wanting earth-friendly homes.

Generating their own electricity is a long-term goal for the pair. "I ultimately want to have a zero-energy house," says Elliot. They have a small 3-kilowatt photovoltaic system that covers some of the home's energy needs. Because photovoltaic panels are costly, he applied for a rebate from the City of Austin, which pays for 50 percent of the cost. Every year he'll continue to add panels to increase the amount of electricity they generate themselves. In the meantime, he's chosen wind energy as his energy source from the local utility company and he's considering getting a slow wind turbine as well.

For Elliot, the chance to design a house for himself was a completely fulfilling experience despite the challenges along the way. He was able to explore and implement a variety of green technologies he's long wanted to try out and incorporated them with his love of the past. For the couple, one of the many benefits of the house is that it transports them, giving them the feeling of living in another era. "I've always wanted to live in a castle," admits Lisa. "This is the next best thing."

Above: Ceiling fans, good cross-ventilation, and cast earth walls that breathe all help to keep the house cool and dry.

Left: The couple's art studio at the front of the house provides anchorage for their Tibetan prayer flags.

1. **CAST EARTH CONSTRUCTION**
Popular in hot climates but workable in cold as well, building with cast earth eliminates the need for wood framing, thus saving trees. It also absorbs moisture and keeps the interior of the house cool.

2. **PHOTOVOLTAIC PANELS**
A 3-kilowatt system on the roof converts the sun's rays into electricity.

3. **SOY-BASED SPRAY-IN INSULTION**
A better alternative than the more commonly used petroleum-based insulation, this bio-base spray is a total fill insulation that boasts better insulating properties than conventional fiberglass.

4. **LOW-E COATED WINDOWS**
Windows with low-emittance coating block heat and UV rays from entering the house.

5. **BLACK WATER SYSTEM**
All of the water used in the house is treated with nontoxic chemicals, then sprayed onto the yard, reducing the need for any additional water for landscaping.

6. **COMPACT FLUORESCENT BULBS**
Compact fluorescent bulbs are in all of the 150 light fixtures in the house, using up to 80 percent less energy than conventional bulbs.

7. **LOW-FLUSH TOILETS AND LOW-FLOW SHOWERHEADS**
Using low-flush toilets and low-flow showerheads reduces water usage by as much as 50 percent.

8. **LOW-VOC PAINTS AND FINISHES**
Low amounts of volatile organic compounds provide cleaner, chemical-free air.

9. **TREE RECYCLING**
Fallen cedars on the lot were reborn as posts for the balconies and side railings on the front walkway.

10. **SALVAGED MATERIALS**
Doors, hardware, and vintage kitchen cabinets were found at local salvage warehouses.

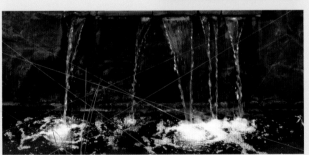

Top: Faux stone is actually made from concrete.

Above left: The soothing waterfall in the front of the house is run on a timer.

Above right: The doors and hardware in the house were found at salvage warehouses.

EXTRAORDINARY EXPERIMENT

McDonough-Trang e-House
Stone Ridge, New York

MY HOUSE IS REALLY JUST A LABORATORY THAT I HAPPEN TO LIVE IN.
— Michael McDonough

The bamboo staircase leads to the bottom of the "light catcher," a twenty-foot-high trapezoidal space with walls of windows that tilt southeast toward the sun to catch the light.

The 2,200-square-foot house located in New York's Hudson Valley was originally conceived to be a small energy-efficient house where Michael McDonough could camp out on the weekends with his wife, Corinne Trang, and their four-year-old daughter, Colette. But the more Michael researched energy-efficient systems, the more he wanted to push the envelope and experiment with green concepts. "I was excited by the new building technologies introduced over the last fifteen years," explains Michael. "It occurred to me that no one had looked at all of them at once by vetting them out and putting them all in one building." Out went his idea for a simple weekend house, and in came the concept of a livable lab.

With his wife's blessing, Michael began designing the house on-line. "Corinne's a chef, so every meal is an experiment—she totally understands the concept." Michael spent a year examining how different systems, from radiant cooling to solar hot water, would interact with one another and work within the framework of the architecture. "The whole house was designed on a Web site, right down to the plumbing fixtures," says Michael. The Web site also allowed Michael to attract the attention of scientists, builders, engineers, environmentalists, and manufacturers, and provided the perfect on-line venue for professionals to share their ideas for the home's research and development. The Web site also lets him control almost every system—lights, humidity level, and heating and cooling systems—on-line. Whether he's in his office in Manhattan or traveling on business, he can check out what the house is doing, control it, and collect data that he shares with other architects and builders in the green community.

To the casual observer, the two-story house—with a high-end chef's kitchen outfitted with bamboo cabinets, an elegant master bath featuring an oversized soapstone Japanese soaking tub, and Zen-like bedrooms—may look completed, but in fact, it's continually evolving and changing. Because the house is Michael's idea lab, "finishing" it isn't really something he's striving for. "When someone comes to visit, if they expect a completed house, they will either be sorely disappointed or very confused," says Michael as we step inside the minimalist, gallery-like space. "I always have to explain that the house is my way of studying green building; it's a long-term testing ground." Michael sees his house as an evolving experiment, although one that provides comfort and contemporary style for his family. "I have to go slowly," he explains. "I have mechanical engineers run simulations that prove on paper that the various systems can work." For example, right now he's installing an underground cistern that collects up to 30,000 gallons of rainwater, about the same size as a small swimming pool, to experiment with multiple applications for well water. The tanks will be insulated and the water used for cooling the house, melting snow on the roof and walkways, irrigating the lawn, or even putting out fires in an emergency. "I'm trying to capture rainwater and use it in as many ways as possible," says Michael.

While all the projects are fascinating to Michael, Corinne and Colette have a totally different take on e-House. "For Michael, the house is a project, but for me it's home," shares Corinne. "I can't wait to go there every weekend." The house is where the busy family reconnects and weekends are spent playing outside with Colette, reading, and eating delicious meals prepared by Corinne. In the kitchen that Michael customized just for her, Corinne is the happiest. "Michael always makes a conscious effort to really involve the client on each project," explains Corinne. "In this case the client was his wife and he did a wonderful job of designing for me." What she wanted most was flexibility; she didn't want to be contained by the kitchen's layout. While the kitchen has roomy fixed stainless-steel countertops along one wall, Michael granted her wish by creating additional moveable countertops that allow her to move freely within the kitchen. Two stainless open shelves on casters let her find pots and pans in a flash, and the butcher block countertops provide extra prep space. Corinne especially loves that the kitchen opens to the living and dining areas, so she's never isolated while she's cooking but instead is able to connect with her family and friends.

From the outside, the house is contemporary, with a strong dose of whimsy and playfulness. The house features jutting sculptural trapezoids, windows that pop out from an exterior wall, and a roof deck accessed via an outdoor stairway that's part of the roof itself. Its angles and geometries are playful and exaggerated. The floating northwest corner is crafted out of locally milled fir painted a deep red—an homage to the Hudson Valley Dutch Colonial barns that pepper the landscape. The color and the association with historical regional architecture tones down the futuristic look of the house, not only allowing it to blend with the wooded landscape, but making it an update on tradition rather than a total departure. The white exterior/interior walls are a complete insulating system made from AAC (autoclaved aerated concrete, a concrete compound mixed with aluminum). By using AAC, Michael increased the thermal properties of the house and its energy efficiency, and decreased the amount of wood needed for framing.

For Michael and his family, there was never any debate about whether to build a sustainable house. "Why would I want to create a building that is inefficient, unimaginative, makes my family sick, and degrades the environment?" Michael's goal is to be green as well as accessible. He believes that the easier it is for people to incorporate eco-friendly materials and technologies, the more likely they'll become mainstream ideas. For example, while solar panels are a popular technology among die-hard environmentalists, he wonders about their feasibility for the average consumer. The long payback period and high cost are real hurdles to overcome. Instead, Michael believes sometimes the easiest approach is also the most efficient. At e-House he could install a wind generator for a cost of $50 to $100,000 but with nearby wind generators in the Mohawk Valley, the local utility company offers an option to choose wind power as their main source of electricity. The house uses little power because of its passive solar siting and radiant cooling and heating systems, so wind power only costs about five dollars extra per month. For Michael, who is studying some of the most complicated and cutting-edge technologies, it's an example of how sometimes simple green choices are just as powerful.

Inspired by how nature and technology interact, Michael planned the home's relationship to the earth, sun, and wind to be at the forefront of the design. "In Eastern religions, there is no sense that technology and nature are separate; they are considered one," explains Michael. "Frank Lloyd Wright saw it the same way; he thought you should design with nature and nature was one with God." Wanting to pick up on those ideals, Michael designed the placement of the windows to

The architect Michael McDonough custom-designed the kitchen for his wife, Corinne Trang, a chef, with all the essentials—movable butcher block shelving, stainless-steel countertops, bamboo cabinets, and plenty of windows.

The walls in the house are made of autoclaved aerated concrete, a green building material. The complete wall system eliminates the need for wood framing and insulation. AAC is resistant to mildew, incredibly strong, and soundproof.

capture sunlight as well as views of the trees as you walk through the house. "The house is constantly inviting nature indoors," he says. Corinne adds, "With all the light and the windows, you're constantly connected to nature."

E-House is their getaway, and both Michael and Corinne didn't want to clutter up the rooms with too many distractions. Instead, their bedroom is designed simply and quietly, with a very low platform bed and no curtains for a minimalist Eastern sensibility. In fact, that sense of calm is evidenced thoughout. The walls are painted white to highlight the beautiful materials he chose, such as soap-stone in the bathroom, bamboo floors, and stainless-steel countertops.

The modern, pared-down aesthetic also works perfectly for life with a young child. Because of the open, airy flow and not too much furniture, Colette has room to really play. "Our daughter moves around the house like it's a playground," says Corinne. "She runs, she jumps, she climbs the stairs, she uses every room." Outdoors, it's the roof deck that most entrances Colette. Through a small doorway between the two stories is an exterior staircase leading to a small deck. It's an Alice in Wonderland feeling to climb up stairs that are literally part of the roof, one of many details that add to the fun, fresh spirit that pervades the architecture. As we stand on the deck, Michael points out the porcelain nonslip tile that can withstand temperatures from minus 20 up to 140 degrees without fracturing. But Corinne points out something even more everlasting, "I've never been so comfortable in any house that I've ever lived in," she says, smiling at her family. "I can't wait to come here every weekend."

The master bedroom hangs over the rest of the house, and because of the giant windows and the room's proximity to the woods, the family calls it the "view catcher."

Below left: The Tokyo-style bathroom has eco-friendly, radiant-heated soapstone floors and an oversize Japanese Ofuro soaking tub.

Below right: Toto water-saving toilets and faucets are used in the home's bathrooms.

Bare wood floors and simple spare furniture create
a feeling of Zen simplicity throughout the house.

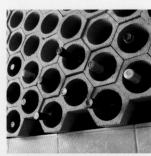

Above left: Architect-home-owner Michael McDonough is also the designer of this award-winning bamboo chair that was named one of the top twenty products of 1998 from *Interior Design* magazine.

Top right: The wine cellar in the basement is kept at a constant temperature of 56 degrees.

Above right: A high-efficiency fireplace helps keep the house warm in the winter.

1. **RUBBLE TRENCH FOUNDATION**
   Because cement requires a lot of fossil fuel to produce, a rubble trench foundation can be a good alternative to a standard concrete foundation, using up to 80 percent less concrete. A rubble trench foundation is made by pouring a two-foot-wide column of gravel in a trench, then placing a large beam made of recycled slag concrete and steel at the top. In the beam, up to 50 percent of the cement is replaced with slag, a waste product from steel production that makes the mixture several times stronger than regular concrete.

2. **AAC WALLS**
   AAC is made by heating aluminum powder, sand, and water. It's lightweight, water vapor permeable, soundproof, fireproof, bulletproof, and resistant to mildew. It uses very little cement and eliminates the need for wood framing and insulation.

3. **RECREATIONAL ROOF DECKS**
   More than 50 percent of the roofs have been designed as tile-paved decks that allow visitors to relax and view the skyline from high atop e-House. These decks are also host to a low-temperature recovered rainwater-based snowmelt system.

4. **PASSIVE SOLAR**
   Instead of situating the house on the traditional east-west axis (long side to the south) common in passive solar design, Michael placed it on a north-south axis (long sides to the east and west) so that every room gets morning and evening sun. By using strategically placed windows in the main area of the house, he maximizes warmth-giving sun and natural daylight. Large roof overhangs prevent too much sun and heat from entering the house in the summer.

5. **IN-FLOOR RADIANT HEATING AND COOLING**
   Tubes carrying hot or cold water run in the floors throughout the house, providing heating or cooling when needed.

6. **OFF-SITE WIND ENERGY**
   Because on-site photovoltaic solar power compares unfavorably with offsite wind energy (PV is inefficient in the northeast and has a long payback period), e-House uses wind power purchased though a local utility company. It costs only about five dollars extra a month to use this alternative energy source.

7. **GEOTHERMAL DEHUMIDIFICATION**
   Underground water (kept at a constant 51 degrees F. by the earth) is pumped through a coil in the house's fresh-air ducts, attracting humidity, removing it from the air, and reducing cooling requirements by 70 percent. This same water that dehumidifies also cools the air, simultaneously.

8. **HIGH-EFFICIENCY LIGHTING**
   Although the house uses low-watt incandescent bulbs throughout, the lighting system also has electronic dimmer controls that substantially reduce energy consumption and extend bulb life. And because the daylighting scheme is so well worked out, almost no artificial light is required during the day.

9. **BAMBOO FLOORING AND KITCHEN CABINETS**
   Bamboo is a renewable resource that matures in three to five years and provides a durable, long-lasting alternative to tropical hardwoods.

10. **LOW-VOC FINISHES, PRIMERS, AND PAINTS**
    To keep the air free of volatile organic compounds that emit toxic gases into the air, all finishes, primers, and paints had low-VOC formulas.

RURAL RETREAT

Wente-Hyland Farmhouse
Millerton, New York

THINKING ABOUT THE ENVIRONMENT, THE WIND, AND SUNLIGHT HAS ALWAYS
BEEN A KEY COMPONENT IN MY WORK.
—Larry Wente

Previous pages, left: The design of this Millerton, New York, house is influenced by the region's historic farmhouses.

Previous pages, right: The gardens, with their architectural grasses, bridge the gap between the formal and wild elements surrounding the home.

It was on an afternoon drive through the backroads of Millerton, New York, that investment banker Jack Hyland and architect Larry Wente noticed a small For Sale sign that changed everything. For almost a decade, the Manhattan-based couple had been happily spending weekends in a pretty, 1920s Colonial in the nearby town of Sharon, Connecticut. They weren't in the market for a new place, had no plans to move, and certainly had no thoughts of building their own house. But the sign's location at the top of a scenic hill where, as Larry describes it, "the whole world opens up," intrigued them.

It took a few trips back, and a ladder, to really get a sense of the land, because the majority of the 41-acre lot was covered with 7-foot-high stalks of corn. But when they climbed to the top of the tallest ladder they could find for a bird's-eye view, they were thrilled to see spectacular vistas in all directions. "What we found was that the views were quite varied," says Larry. "To the east there's a view of Indian Lake and Indian Mountain, to the south you can see twenty-five-miles down the valley with a hillside range on each side, and to the west is a series of ridges and an agricultural field." For the first time in his career, Larry was ready to build a house for himself. Within weeks they had sold their Colonial, bought the land, and begun dreaming up plans for their new house.

For Larry, who has long practiced sustainable architecture as a partner with Manhattan-based Gertler Wente Kerbeykian Architects, there was no question that he would build their new house green. "It's simply the way I was trained," he explains. "Thinking about the environment, the wind, and sunlight has always been a key component in my work." One of their first green decisions was to keep the majority of the land as a working farm, hiring a local farmer to manage 35 acres of corn and alfalfa fields.

There were no trees, only corn, on the property, so Larry and Jack knew they would have some planting to do to create a lush backdrop for their new home. Luckily, an abandoned nursery across the road had beautiful spruce and white pine trees as well as midsize maples they were able to rescue. "We moved approximately one hundred thirty trees," Jack says, pointing out how the trees provide the house with a windbreak from the valley's strong winds. After they'd planted their scavenged trees, a local orchard was sold, and they were able to purchase and rescue thirty-one twenty-year-old apple trees, including Fuji, Macoun, and Red Delicious, for their very own working orchard.

With an instant apple crop dotting their landscape, it's only appropriate that Jack and Larry decided to build an eco farmhouse. The historically agricultural region influenced the home's design and the house takes its visual cues from the nearby farmhouses that dot the landscape. Located right in the middle of the Coleman Station Historic District, Larry and Jack's property is surrounded by a dozen or so houses and barns that date back to the 1700s. "We wanted to be good neighbors," explains Larry. "So we based the design on some of the nearby barn structures with the ad hoc approach of a house that was added to over time." Like barns that are oriented along a north-south axis to capture summer breezes for livestock, the central artery of the house is a long, narrow north-south structure with an additional tower on one side that looks like an abstracted silo.

The colors of the home's exterior materials meld beautifully with the landscape. Green-painted cedar siding on the house distinguishes it from the natural cedar of the tower.

A ribbon strip of windows next to the living room lets sunlight pour into a long hallway, blurring the line between indoors and out. The house, long and narrow, maximizes cross-breezes. Radiant heating extends beyond the floors to the stone wall at the front of the house, which enables the homeowners to lower the thermostat by up to four degrees.

Sliding glass doors connect the master
bathroom with a roomy deck.

Following pages: Architect-homeowner Larry Wente gazes southwest to the distant farmland of historic Dutchess County, New York. Large windows in the modern, barnlike home make the indoors and outdoors seem like one. The lattice atop these giant windows minimizes summertime heat by filtering the sun's rays.

Right: The kitchen cabinets and island countertops were crafted out of eye-catching anigre wood, which is certified for being harvested from a sustainable forest.

Below: The dining room combines sustainable woods and limestone from local quarries.

Above: The sun porch beyond the kitchen is convertible for year-round use. In the summertime, screen walls replace the glass.

Right: The limestone wall features radiant heat.

Far right: All of the home's furnishings are made from natural materials, such as stone, metal, glass, and wood, for an intentional handcrafted look.

Opposite: The silo-shaped tower, with its small loft bedroom, affords brilliant views and helps to vent the hot air through the uppermost windows.

Opposite, above left: The bed in the guest bedroom dates from the 1850s and was designed by British architect Charles Eastlake. Homeowner Larry Wente purchased it at an antique shop in Williamstown, Massachusetts.

Opposite, above right: The guest bedrooms utilize antique beds that are retrofitted to accept modern-sized mattresses.

Opposite, bottom: The balcony is accessible from the master bathroom or bedroom. Tiles on the bathroom floor are in a four-foot-square grid, designed to reduce construction waste since most materials already come in this size. Douglas fir frames this space; the large beams were reclaimed from old buildings and are held together by wooden pegs.

Locally milled limestone frames the doorways and windows. "In the summer the green allows the house to blend in with the trees and in the winter the cedar blends in with the bark," explains Larry about his color choices. Additionally, he chose a deep green shade, not only to mimic the prevalent color of nearby barns, but to make a statement as well. "We liked the idea of painting a 'green' house green," Larry says. For the interior, a subtle color palette works to frame and highlight exterior views. The cool gray of the living room contrasts with the warm pale maple cabinets, while richer mustard yellows and reds warm up north-facing rooms.

When designing the interior, Larry's main goal was to capture the picturesque views as one moves through the house. An abundance of windows in the home blur the line between indoors and out. When you step into the living room and catch sight of the corner row of sloping windows, the views and the light are so surreal and breathtaking you feel as if you're inside a landscape painting of endless sky and valley. These gorgeous views carry throughout the house, with each room and every corner revealing a new vista—whether it's the borrowed landscape of the mountainside or their own lush gardens.

Jack, an avid gardener, designed the quarter acre of gardens to enrich the landscape around the house throughout the year. In the early summer, a long allée of nepeta gives the gardens a bluish-purple cast. In July and August, the strong yellows of rudbeckia highlight the pool. As summer progresses, the dozen or so different ornamental grasses, which were cut to the ground in March, have grown back and dominate the gardens. By late summer there are purple-hued beds of tall, slender stalks of *Verbena bonariensis* and

arched trellises covered in blossoming blue morning glories. These mix dramatically with a huge bed of goldenrod and mounds of white autumn clematis that trail along a fence. In the winter the trellises bring architectural interest to the garden, and a 100-yard path of tall, narrow arborvitae called Degroot's Spire, a native replacement for Italian cypress, provides elegant greenery.

To keep the spotlight on the outside scenery, the interior spaces benefit from a skillful blend of classic and contemporary elements that are both elegant and serene. Family heirlooms such as a circa nineteenth-century needlepoint rug share space with black leather and metal cinema chairs based on a 1950s design. There are no loud patterns or attention-grabbing furniture styles here. Instead, everything—from the classic grand piano to the chic boxy white sofa—invites guests to relax and take it all in. The living room's crisp black-and-white palette is softened by all the wood throughout the space—stained poplar along the angled wall, western red cedar on the sloped ceiling, and Forest Stewardship Council–certified anigre (an African hardwood) cabinets that hide the TV behind a cabinet that looks like a sliding barn door. The bedrooms have an updated country feel, with antique painted bed frames, Oriental carpets, and assorted American antique desks, armoires, and side tables. In the eco spirit of reusing and repurposing, all the furniture—with the exception of a dining table they had custom made from salvaged pine attic boards—were brought from an old house.

Larry and Jack's elegant aesthetic even extends to the green features of the house. Rather than put the photovoltaic panels, which provide up to two-thirds of the home's energy needs, on the roof, Larry opted to put them in

Above left: Variegated honeysuckle produces flowers in the summer and berries in the fall.

Above right: Pink Japanese anemone grow on 2- to 3-foot stems in a grass bed that contains red grasses and perennials.

Far left: The forty-foot rill is filled with carp, and it ends in a garden of black bamboo (*Phyllostachys nigra*). Four cement English fence posts in obelisk form surround a gravel path that crosses the rill. 'Sweet Kate' apple trees, *Hostas,* and *Tradescantia* line the water. To the far right is black fountain grass (*Pennisetum* 'Moudry'). In the back are Norwegian spruce, 'Karl Foerster' grasses, and white allium.

Left: Amaranthus atropurpureus (annual) is in the foreground at left; black elephant ears (*Colocasia esculenta* 'Black Magic') and varieties of hosta are to the right.

Below: The glassed-in porch is a favorite viewing spot for the changing weather and seasonal plants. Inside the morning glory–covered tuteurs are lavender and salvia, surrounded by 'Karl Foerster' grasses. Next to the wall is fountain grass *Pennisetum* 'Hamlyn'). To the right is a row of European hornbeam, and the meadow is filled with goldenrod.

one of the gardens, amid native grasses and flowers. "I don't find them attractive on the roof," admits Larry. "So I wanted to have them in the garden like sculpture." The passive cooling system is even more subtle. With no air-conditioning, the house relies on a series of ground-level casement windows that draw in cool air. He based the concept on the fact that air at ground level is very cool even in the summer. "By opening up windows close to the ground you capture the air current," explains Larry. Fans circulate the air and open windows in the tower pull hot air out of the house. The breezes feel crisp and constant. Larry himself is surprised with how effectively it works. "Even on the hottest days of the summer it's cool inside," he states. In the winter months, radiant heating underneath the concrete floors and in the limestone walls keeps the house toasty.

The house also has an abundance of recycled elements that don't stand out as green. Part of the frame comes from salvaged wood from a New England barn. The tiles in the bathrooms are crafted out of recycled glass. All the tiles in the kitchen were fished out of the remainder bins of a local tile manufacturer. It took repeated trips to find all the tiles he needed, but Larry preferred using pieces left over from other jobs rather than ordering new. Even the stone lintels over the windows are from a local salvage warehouse.

For Larry and Jack, the biggest surprise came from how easy the whole process has been. From their chance sighting of the For Sale sign, to selling their Colonial right away, to a painless construction process, there's been little of the stress that so many people encounter when they build a new house. "It's by far the smoothest building process that I've ever been involved in," says Larry, who knows firsthand how challenging any new construction can be. "It's hard to believe, but I wouldn't change anything."

The pergola adjacent to the home's long and narrow pool keeps bathers out of the sun and frames the view of the lake beyond.

Top: The house has no air-conditioning—the green cooling system works with ground-level windows that draw in the cooler air, ceiling fans that circulate it, and high windows that let the warm air out.

Bottom: The panels next to the front door are light switches reminiscent of those in nineteenth-century American farmhouses

1. **LOCAL CONTRACTORS AND MATERIALS**
   To support local businesses and reduce the need for driving long distances—which wastes fuel and produces greenhouse gases—all of the workers, from the stonemason to the millworker to the contractor, live within a five-mile radius of the house. Materials including the stone from the stone entrywall and fireplaces were from local sources.

2. **SOLAR PANELS**
   Photovoltaic panels in the garden convert the sun's rays into energy, supplying about two-thirds of the home's electricity needs. The rest is provided by the local utility company.

3. **REDUCTION OF CONSTRUCTION WASTE**
   In order to produce less construction waste, the house was designed on a four-foot-module grid to accommodate the many construction materials that come in four-foot increments.

4. **RECYCLED MATERIALS**
   Recycled materials included recycled glass tiles, timber salvaged from a New Hampshire barn, and salvaged stone lintels.

5. **FSC-CERTIFIED WOOD**
   All the new wood in the house was from forests that are certified by the Forest Stewardship Council as practicing sustainable harvesting and growth practices. Douglas fir was used for framing the exterior,

and anigre wood was used for the cabinets in the kitchen and living room.

6. **GRAY WATER SYSTEM**
   All roof rainwater is collected, filtered, and reused for irrigation.

7. **RADIANT-HEAT FLOORING AND WALLS**
   Hydronic radiant heating underneath the concrete floors and through the limestone wall at the front of the house is a very efficient form of heat that allows the thermostats to be set, on average, five degrees lower than conventional heating systems.

8. **NO AC**
   The house relies instead on a passive cooling system. Ground-level awning windows draw cooler ground temperature air in, fans circulate the air, and high windows in the silo-like tower vent it out again. A curved wooden lattice awning outside the living room provides additional shade.

9. **CONCRETE FLOORS**
   On the first level, concrete floors warmed by the sun release their heat for hours during the day.

10. **REUSING FURNITURE**
    Every piece of furniture, with the exception of the dining table—crafted from salvaged attic boards—was brought from their old house, eliminating the need to buy new pieces.

COUNTRY CHIC

Grier-Steckler Saltbox
Columbia County,
New York

I WAS LOOKING FOR SOMETHING A LITTLE MORE MODERN; MICHELE WAS LOOKING FOR
SOMETHING HISTORICAL, SO [DENNIS] GAVE A CLASSIC SALTBOX ALL THESE MODERN
RIGHT ANGLES BY CUTTING IT IN TWO.
—Cathy Grier

When musician Cathy Grier and Broadway producer Michele Steckler hired architect Dennis Wedlick to build their house in Columbia County, New York, the first thing he did was give them an assignment. He asked the couple to go home and write down all the things they wanted in their new house without thinking about cost, practicality, or even each other. After decades as one of the country's most sought after architects, Dennis was savvy enough to know that trying to merge individual visions of the perfect home can be a recipe for couples counseling. Instead, he advised them to keep their real estate fantasies to themselves until they met with him again the following week with their lists in hand.

The duo diligently followed his directions, and didn't even peek at each other's lists lest they interfere with Dennis's creative process. Cathy was passionate about building green, interested in lessening their impact on the earth, and concerned about the health hazards of certain materials. Michele wanted to wake up to morning sun. They both asked for separate guest quarters. "We wanted guests to feel like they have their own private space when they visit us," says Cathy, who often plays host to family and friends. Michele, who grew up in a Colonial home, also asked for a place that would offer a nod to historical design and provide a complementary backdrop for her collection of antique furniture and rugs. "Michele has a love of beautiful old country things," says Cathy, whose decidedly different fantasy aesthetic was more modern and pared down with clean lines and light-filled rooms—not something most historic homes can boast. Cathy's love of minimalism even extended to the closets; she asked Dennis to limit their number so she wouldn't be tempted to amass clutter.

After much discussion, Dennis came up with a design that brilliantly manages to fuse their distinctive visions into a passive solar house that suits them both to a tee. His solution was to take a traditional saltbox design and literally cut the house right down the middle, placing the two sides at right angles to each other, with the back corners connecting. A windowed living room between the two wings acts as a bridge. It's a fresh, tongue-in-cheek spin on tradition that's modern without ignoring the past. The home's historical influence makes it contextual to an area where century-old farmhouses and Colonial homes preside.

Sited to take advantage of passive solar energy, the home faces southwest, maximizing solar gain. In the winter the sun shines in, but structural overhangs from the roof keep the heat of the summer sun out. The clever design also takes full advantage of 360-degree views of their land and the rolling hills beyond. One wing features the master bed and bath on the second floor, with the kitchen and dining areas below. To get to the second wing, which is home to the guest room that doubles as Cathy's music studio and a first-floor study, you only have to walk through the sun-filled central living room.

"We were so blown away," says Cathy about Dennis's design. "It just made so much sense. I was looking for something a little more modern; Michele was looking for something historical, so he gave a classic saltbox all these modern right angles by cutting it in two." Adds the associate architect on the project, Carol Gretter, "They are two very unique personalities, and having two individual structures coming together was reflective of that."

The owner's antique pieces, such as this Oriental carpet, are given an automatic update when paired with more current designs like a boxy cream sofa and crisp roman shades.

The kitchen countertops were crafted from maple and birch trees that had to be cut down when the house was built.

For the interior, the couple chose a soft but glowing palette of low-VOC pale green, golden yellow, and beige paints that worked with the New England light.

The homeowners used a maple tree cut from their own property for this kitchen counter. They had it milled, wanting the tree to have a second life in their home.

The interior has a beautiful simplicity. Unfussy and tightly edited, the rooms have all the necessities without anything extraneous. Clean-lined antiques and lighting with graphic profiles are found in every room. Many of the older pieces are presents from Michele's antique dealer parents, including the Oriental carpets. Their stately four-poster wood bed frame came from a Massachusetts store that retrofits antique beds to current sizes. More interested in design than pedigree, they even hit local yard sales, scoring for one dollar a pair of Shaker chairs in need of rehabbing.

To keep all the antiques from making the house seem too staid, an understated color scheme modernizes the space. Upholstery and bedding were kept neutral in beiges, browns, and whites, creating a soothing flow from one room to the next. Taking cues from the landscape, they opted for hues that work with the light and the ever-changing New England seasons, such as ultra-pale greens, warm beiges, and a rich golden shade in the bedroom. Even the artwork presents a link to nature: the few paintings on display are pretty landscapes that capture breathtaking pastoral scenes.

When they had to buy new, Cathy and Michele chose sleek yet understated pieces like a Mitchell Gold chaise made from sustainable wood without formaldehyde. They found a local lighting designer who makes everything on site, and added a mix of antique-inspired iron chandeliers and more current pendant bulbs. Their custom kitchen countertops were crafted of the maple and birch trees they had to remove to build the house. The cherry cabinets and columns of drawers were planned with all of their cooking gear in mind, so every single piece has its place.

It was the bucolic region, two hours from Manhattan, that lured the couple away from the city where they'd lived for the previous decade. They fell hard for the region's rolling hills, strong sense of community, and easy accessibility to Manhattan's cultural offerings. "It's as close to perfection as you can get," explains Cathy. But while they knew they wanted a foothold in the area, they were uncertain of exactly what that would be. One afternoon they would search for land and the next they would be touring old farmhouses. One morning while walking through a 14-acre piece of land everything instantly came into focus. "We really felt like this would be a wonderful place to live, we just knew," says Cathy.

It was Cathy who really drove the green focus of the house, researching every book, Web site, and article she could find on building a healthy sustainable home. She shared the information she found with Dennis as well as their contractor. "I was just going by my nose," Cathy remembers. "I just kept Googling things. I would type in 'healthy home,' 'green home,' 'sustainable kitchen,' whatever word combination I could think of that might help me learn more." She quickly came up with areas to focus on—examining the health implications of everything they put in the house, buying locally, and trying to purchase sustainable and recyclable products.

Cathy was surprised to find several health hazards in products commonly used on job sites. First, she learned that foundations are often sealed with a petroleum-based product that could have links to cancer, so she went with a healthier rubber-based seal. Then she discovered that most paints contain VOCs (volatile organic compounds), toxic chemicals that off-gas into the air. She was thrilled to

learn that Benjamin Moore offers many shades in a low-VOC version called Eco Spec. For insulation, the couple chose a formaldehyde-free fiberglass for the walls, blue jean insulation for the ceiling, and recycled paper for one attic. When it came time to finish the kitchen cabinets, Cathy discovered that instead of polyurethane they could use natural tung oil, a cleansing oil from the nuts of the tung tree. It provides a glowing, low-gloss finish and is a moisture-proof sealant.

During the building process the couple tried to recycle as much construction waste as possible. "I would be in the bin fishing out every bit of scrap wood I could find." Cathy says with a chuckle. From the scraps alone, they built a garden shed and eight wine bins. While Cathy was vigilant about trying to make the best choices possible, she also realized

that compromises had to be made. "I hated that so many books said that if you're going to build green it has to be like this," she states. "I don't believe in that. Sometimes you have to make choices. For instance, we wanted to use recycled flooring, but it was too expensive, so we went with certified pine and that's okay." She hopes people will realize that even small changes can have huge impacts. "Just orienting your house to take advantage of passive solar can reduce your energy bills by ten percent and it won't cost you a dime more," she says. Even the size of their house was a conscious effort to lesson their energy usage, an impact she's aware of every day. "To lower our footprint we went with a twenty-one-hundred-square-foot space and that's all the house we'll ever need," says Cathy happily.

Above left: Buying everything locally was imperative to the owners; they found early-American reproduction lighting and chandeliers within a two-hour drive at Authentic Design.

Above right: The reproduction clawfoot tub is the perfect height for soaking in the treetop views.

Opposite: A nearby company in Massachusetts retrofits antique beds, such as this four-poster, to fit current mattress sizes.

Right: The house is oriented southwest for passive solar gain. Structural overhangs on the roof block out the hot summer sun but let the low winter sun flood into the house during the colder months.

Below: An Adirondack chair takes in the glorious views of Columbia County's rolling hills.

GREEN FEATURES

1. **NONPETROLEUM PRODUCT FOUNDATION**
   The house uses a rubber-based product that provides a nontoxic moisture-proof sealant for concrete foundations.

2. **CELLULOSE INSULATION**
   To avoid formaldehyde and its off-gassing potentially dangerous chemicals, in the attic they went with nontoxic cellulose insulation that's made from recycled newspapers.

3. **RECYCLED CONSTRUCTION WASTE**
   They saved scrap wood and used it to build wine bins and a garden shed.

4. **PASSIVE SOLAR**
   The home faces southwest to maximize passive solar gain. A structural overhang keeps summer sun out and lets low winter sun in.

5. **HOT-WATER RADIANT-HEAT SYSTEM**
   Instead of forced air, which encourages dust and mold, they kept their air cleaner by opting for radiators that heat with hot water.

6. **ULTRA-EFFICIENT BOILER**
   A gas-fired high-efficiency condensing wall-mounted boiler is 98 percent efficient, saving money and gas.

7. **RECYCLED CLEARED TREES**
   While they had to cut down a few maple and birch trees to make room for the house, they had a cabinet-maker craft the logs into a sturdy kitchen worktable and counters.

8. **NONTOXIC WOOD FINISHES**
   To finish their flooring, they chose tung oil for a beautiful nontoxic finish.

9. **LOW-VOC PAINTS AND FINISHES**
   Benjamin Moore's Eco Spec low-VOC paints were used throughout the house.

10. **FSC-CERTIFIED WOOD**
    By choosing wood certified by the Forest Stewardship Council, they ensured that the wood came from sustainable forests.

Above left: A rain chain helps to guide water from the built-in roof gutter to an underground pipe.

Above right: The red door with its rope handle is the entrance to a small gardening shed on the property.

WOODLAND HIDEAWAY

Hughey-Clancy Residence
Dutchess County, New York

WE WANTED OUR HOUSE TO BE A REALLY MUSCULAR BUILDING. REALLY
MASCULINE, SIMPLE, AND STRONG. THE OPPOSITE OF THE VICTORIAN FUSSY
AND DECORATIVE STYLE.

—Barbara Hughey

Previous pages, left: For a chemical-free alternative to paint, pigments derived from powdered stone were mixed with plaster to tint all the walls a vibrant yellow.

Previous pages, right: An electric-blue Adirondack chair adds a pop of color to the screened-in porch.

"We were going for a major change," says Barbara Hughey with a laugh, explaining how she and her husband, Dennis Clancy, ended up swapping their nineteenth-century Victorian home located in the quaint town of Rhinebeck, New York, for a new green house set in a wooded 25-acre property. Although only a few miles apart, "the two houses are almost polar opposites," says Barbara. The couple's airy, light-filled house with cathedral ceilings, abundant windows, and concrete floors is light-years away from the warren of small rooms and even smaller windows that are a hallmark of Victorian architecture. Hughey, a landscape designer, and Clancy, a former pilot, adored their antique home, but when the opportunity to start fresh presented itself, they decided to embrace an entirely new aesthetic. "We wanted our house to be a really muscular building," explains Barbara about their vision. "Really masculine, simple, and strong. The opposite of the Victorian fussy and decorative style."

Barbara and Dennis, both ardent environmentalists, were initially drawn to the land because of its total privacy. Drawing on Barbara's professional knowledge, their first goal was to do an ecological restoration project, hoping to rescue what they could from a scourge of invasive plants. "The Nature Conservancy is often quoted as saying that invasive plants are the second greatest risk to the environment," warns Barbara. For Barbara and Dennis, their call to action came when they couldn't walk through their property because the invasive honeysuckle, grapevine, and garlic mustard had grown so thick. To get rid of the predatory plants that rob native species of sun, soil, light, and nutrients, they went through the arduous process of removing the invasive plants by their roots and burning them. The payoff took a few years, but

acre by acre the native plants, ferns, morel mushrooms, witch hazel, and dogwood trees began to thrive. "It was so satisfying to see," exclaims Barbara proudly.

When it came time to design the house, Barbara and Dennis made the enlightened decision to build a place that would complement, rather than stand out from, the landscape. "I think it shows respect for the place you inhabit, not to mention the neighbors," states Barbara. "In my opinion it's more interesting to be pleasantly surprised when you enter the house and see how substantial and pretty it is inside, while outdoors nature takes center stage." To that end, they went with subtle soft beige stucco and a dark brownish gray tin roof—colors that reflected the look of the woods in the winter. Local architect Susan Sie gave the two-story, three-bedroom house an understated exterior design, and, just as the couple wanted, the wow factor happens as soon as you step inside. A white pine cathedral ceiling draws the eye upward in the light-filled space, exposed steel I-beams add drama above the hearth, and the windows are all poised to frame stellar views of the woods, the beautiful 2,000-square-foot gardens, or the Catskill Mountains in the distance.

The couple opted for a modern take on mountain lodge style with plush furniture, natural materials, and a striking fireplace crafted from salvaged boards of a grapejuice vat, which anchors the living area. Before the move, they donated or sold all of their old pieces, knowing that what worked in their Victorian home probably wouldn't flatter a more contemporary backdrop. To summon the woodsy retreat vibe they were going for, Barbara and Dennis stayed with materials found in nature—cotton upholstery, wool rugs,

The concrete floor, which covers the radiant-heating coils, was cut with a saw to give it the appearance of stone. For a nontoxic, chemical-free alternative to paint, Barbara and Dennis mixed natural stone pigments in powder form with a gypsum-based plaster to tint the walls a happy shade of yellow.

wicker and wood furniture. They chose pieces that encourage lounging, such as an over-stuffed white sofa with tons of pillows, roomy wicker armchairs from the 1920s, and an iconic Le Corbusier black leather chaise. To keep the home feeling peaceful and airy, there's no clutter or excess. Every piece has a purpose, from the sleek mid-century dining chairs picked up in a Millerton, New York, antiques shop to the drum pendant light hand-printed with a vine pattern that echoes the greenery outside.

Although the couple wanted an open floor plan on the first floor to flow the kitchen, dining, and living areas together, they use area rugs and architectural features to give each space distinction. When you enter the house, the airy foyer leads you toward the kitchen, an L-shaped space that is anchored by a vintage table by a local Rhinebeck artist. Barbara loves the stock maple cabinets for their simplicity. "They were the cleanest design we could find," she explains. Dennis handcrafted the countertops from poured concrete, and added an element of surprise by embedding vintage clock gears into the surface. "I love working on it; the counter is so handsome and incredibly strong," says Barbara.

Just across the hall is the dining area centered along a rectangular row of windows with pretty green trim flanked by two antique Chinese screens. Dennis carved the gorgeous table out of a single piece of oak, and its simple, strong lines are beautifully paired with the sculptural curves of 1940s Danish modern chairs. The combination of a drum pendant centered over the table and a pale green antique carpet below helps to define the dining area.

Upstairs, the three bedrooms share the same relaxed and comfortable aesthetic as the public spaces. The master bedroom is enlivened by the richly patterned coverlet and textile wall hangings made by a microbanking co-op of female artisans in India. "It really meant something to us to buy pieces that support women," says Barbara. The room's yellow walls offer a neutral background for the deep reds, chocolates, and yellows in both the bedding and the art. The third bedroom has been turned into an office, but just in case they need a break, Barbara added the elegant Le Corbusier chaise. In the outdoor rooms—the upstairs sleeping porch and the screened porch downstairs—the landscape is meant to be the main attraction, and Barbara kept the focus on the native setting by decorating simply with Adirondack and canvas director's chairs.

The palette throughout the house is muted and subtle. For the interior walls they used a gypsum-based plaster made specifically to work with AAC (autoclaved aerated concrete—a concrete compound mixed with aluminum), the green building material for the house. They avoided paints all together, preferring to color the plaster with nontoxic natural stone pigments. To get just the right soft hues, they worked with a decorative artist who mixed small samples with pigments from Kremer, a shop in Manhattan, to create a soothing pale yellow shade to use throughout the house. "The color brightens up a snowy landscape in the winter and blends with the deep greens of summer," explains Barbara. Pale green trim highlights the windows and the vistas. "We wanted those windows to look like art," says Barbara. She adds, "The colors and the views make the house feel enormously peaceful."

For Barbara and Dennis, there was never a thought of building any way except green. "We feel that it's morally very compelling and politically very wise to lesson our impact on

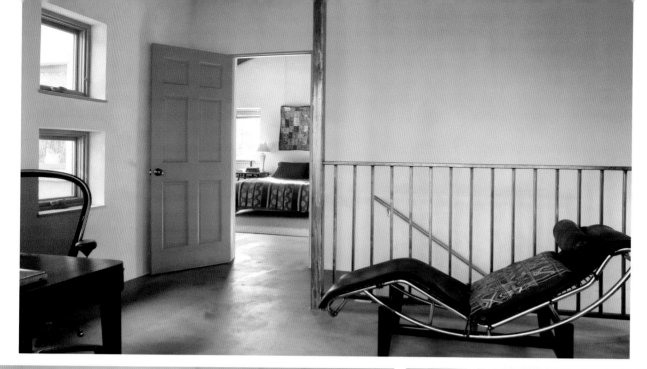

Top and above: The multicolored bedspread, wall hangings, and pillows in the bedroom and on the chair in the hall were handcrafted by female artisans in India.

Right: Polished concrete floors finished with charcoal pigment are an excellent conductor for radiant-heat flooring.

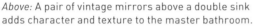

Above: A pair of vintage mirrors above a double sink adds character and texture to the master bathroom.

Right: Owner Barbara Clancy kept all the windows free of curtains to spotlight the views so that each vista looks like a painting.

the planet," explains Barbara, and adds, "It's also smart economically." Dennis, a vegan for twenty-five-years, wanted their house to be an extension of his devotion to healthy living. He made sure every material and substance used, from nontoxic wood finishes to the cleaning materials, were ultra clean and environmentally friendly.

Dennis was particularly intrigued by the energy efficiency and nontoxic properties of AAC. The light but incredibly strong concrete compound comes in twelve-inch-thick blocks two feet in length and eight-inches high, and is used in place of a wood frame, insulation, and a subfloor. It's a perfect material to pair with a radiant-heat flooring system. "It buffers the temperature beautifully," explains Barbara. "It's an incredible feeling walking on warm floors."

The couple's adventurous spirit didn't stop at the material they chose for their home; they also made the decision to be their own general contractors. Their biggest challenge as contractors? "Getting everyone acquainted with an innovative material," says Barbara. "No one had worked with AAC before." But the AAC gave the couple a few opportunities that wouldn't be available otherwise. One of the biggest was the chance to use stucco for the exterior walls, which gives the house an earthy Southwestern feel. "In the Northeast it would be unwise to stucco a wood-framed house because it would break down," explains Barbara. "But in this case, it bonds with the structural element of the building, which is AAC, not wood."

When we ask Barbara what her favorite aspect of the house is, she answers immediately. "The light," she exclaims. The house is oriented for passive solar, and the southern exposure means that light streams through the house year-round. "The light in the house is just beautiful all the time."

GREEN FEATURES

1. ELIMINATED INVASIVE PLANTS
Nutrient- and sunlight-robbing plants like honeysuckle and grapevine were removed by their roots and burned, allowing native dogwood and ferns to return.

2. AAC
Autoclaved aerated concrete is a compound made by mixing aluminum and concrete. It's nontoxic and has excellent thermal properties. It's an extremely energy-efficient material. Using AAC also eliminates the need for wood framing and insulation.

3. INSULATING ROOF
There are six-inches of insulation between the exposed pine roof and the tin roof to increase the thermal properties of the house.

4. PASSIVE SOLAR
The house faces due south. In the winter the low sun floods the house with sunlight and the AAC with warmth. In the summer, roof overhangs keep the heat out.

5. RADIANT-HEAT FLOORING
There is no need for forced air heating in the house because hot water runs through tubes underneath the floor, heating the polished concrete floor.

6. FURNACE
Ninety-eight percent of the gas is converted into heat.

7. NO AC
The house is sited underneath several trees that provide the house with welcome shade. Well-placed windows provide cross-ventilation enhanced by ceiling fans, eliminating the need for air-conditioning. The AAC also keeps the house temperate.

8. NATURAL PIGMENTS
Pigments derived from powdered stone were mixed with a gypsum-based plaster to tint the walls in a completely natural and chemical-free way.

9. RECYCLED MATERIALS
The fireplace mantel is made of boards from a vintage grape juice vat. Repurposing salvaged materials is a great way to recycle.

10. ALL-NATURAL CLEANERS AND FINISHES
All the cleaning materials are biodegradable and all natural. Wood cabinets and tables were finished with a nontoxic water-based finish. Concrete floors were polished and finished with charcoal pigment.

Dennis Clancy embedded vintage clock gears into the concrete countertops he made himself.

RESOURCES

ARCHITECTS AND DESIGNERS

URBAN PRESERVATION
Gleicher Design Group
www.gleicherdesign.com
Interior Designer: David Barry

NEWLYWED NEST
Chris Cobb
CF Architecture
www.cfarchitecture.com

OCEAN BREEZE
David Hertz
David Hertz Architects Inc.,
Studio of Environmental Architecture
www.studioea.com
Interior Designer:
Joe Lucas, Parrish Chilcoat
Lucas Studio
www.lucasstudioinc.com

THE ALLEY BOX
Jim Barger
Greenleaf Construction, Inc.
www.greenleafconst.net
Interior Designer:
Jonathan Mathews, Kwanchai Design
www.kwanchai.net

ROYAL RENOVATION
Stuart Silk
Stuart Silk Architects
www.stuartsilk.com

PARADISE BY THE SEA
Kaizer Talib
Urban Form Design
228 North Andrews Ave.
Fort Lauderdale, FL 33301
www.urbanformdesign.com

SIDE BY SIDE
Travis Young
Studio Momentum Architects
www.studiomomentum.com

SIMPLY MODERN
Maryann Thompson
Maryann Thompson Architects
www.maryannthompson.com

SUN HOME
Tonino Vicari
Tectonic Design
http://tectonic-design.com/index.html

FROM THE ASHES
David Goldberg
Mithun
www.mithun.com

CLIFF DWELLERS
Rod Freebairn
Freebairn-Smith & Craine
www.f-sc.com

ECOMANOR
William Harrison
Harrison Design Associates
www.harrisondesignassociates.com
Interior Designer:
Jillian Pritchard-Cooke
DES-SYN
www.des-syn.com/pressroom/cooke.html

UP IN THE TREETOPS
Elliot Johnson
Images Of …
www.imagesof.net

EXTRAORDINARY EXPERIMENT
Michael McDonough
Michael McDonough Architect
www.michaelmcdonough.com

RURAL RETREAT
Larry Wente
Gertler and Wente Architects
www.gwkarch.com

COUNTRY CHIC
Dennis Wedlick
Dennis Wedlick Architect
www.denniswedlick.com/home.html

WOODLAND HIDEAWAY
Susan Sie
Sie Designs
845.876.0510

Sharkey-Gleicher
URBAN PRESERVATION

Paints
Interior Latex Coating paints minimize negative impacts on air quality because they are low odor and have zero or low VOCs (volatile organic compounds). Sherwin-Williams: www.sherwin-williams.com

High-Efficiency Boiler
Weil-McLain ultra condensing high-efficiency 230 gas boiler and Ultra Plus 80 indirect fired hot water heater is 98 percent efficient for a low-temperature application. Weil-McLain: 219-879-6561; www.weil-mclain.com

Floor Joists, Studs, and Subfloors
Microllam LVL, TimberStrand, and TJ-Performance Plus floor joists, studs, and subfloors are made from easily regener-ated, small-diameter aspen and poplar trees. All three products are manufac-tured from logs that are formed into veneer or strands, then bound together with an adhesive containing no urea-formaldehyde. Weyerhaeuser iLevel: www.ilevel.com

Flooring
The floors are made of Lyptus, a plantation-grown hybrid of the eucalyp-tus tree that matures in just fourteen to sixteen years. The renewable, high-yield hardwood is grown on well-managed plantations, which dedicate one-third of the area to the preservation of native vegetation and intersperse indigenous trees to preserve the natural habitat. Weyerhaeuser: 800-525-5440; http://www.weyerhaeuser.com/our businesses/buildingproducts/ buildingmaterials/ourproducts/lyptus/

Central Vacuum System
The HEPA central vacuum system suppresses 99 percent of all the dust particles. Paired with a ventilation system, it keeps the house dust, mold, and allergen free. Beam; www.beamvac.com

Fireplace
This open-hearth wood-burning Bellfires fireplace is so efficient that after burning about three cords of wood, only a small cupful of ashes remains. The entire flue is wrapped in Cera Foil insulation, safe-guarding the home. It was installed by East End Chimney. www.bellfiresusa.com; www.eastendchimney.com

Appliances
Refrigerator, dishwasher, double convection oven, warming drawer, gas cooktop, kitchen exhaust hood, microwave, clothes washer, and gas clothes dryer are all Energy Star compliant, boasting significant reduction in energy and water use. Bosch: 800-944-2904; www.boschappliances.com.

Closets
California Closets built all the closet systems with an eco-friendly low-emittance particleboard with no urea-formaldehyde. California Closets: 800-274-6574; www.caliclosets.com

Insulation
CertainTeed fiberglass building insula-tion with MemBrain Smart Vapor Retarder forms a barrier that prevents water vapor from condensing within the exterior wall cavity, inhibiting water damage, mold, and mildew. To reduce the amount of energy needed to heat and cool the house and limit noise transmission, the house is insulated below the roof, exterior walls, interior partitions, and floors. CertainTeed: 800-233-8990; www.certainteed.com

Chemical-Free Plywood
The kitchen cabinets, bookcases, and bathroom vanities are made with Columbia Forest Products PureBond hardwood plywood that uses a formaldehyde-free adhesive, improving indoor air quality. Columbia Forest Products: 800-237-2428; www.columbiaforestproducts.com

Interior Plaster
American Clay, www.americanclay.com American Clay is a practical, nontoxic, environmentally friendly, and stylish way to cover your walls. It is also easy to apply and is colored with natural-mineral pigments.

Water Filtration System
All the water that enters the house is filtered via an EcoWater filtration system located in the basement. The system removes 95 percent of the impurities in the water and softens it as well. EcoWater ERR 3000 Water Refiner and ERO 375 Drinking Water System; www.ecowater.com

Marmoleum Flooring
Forbo Marmoleum flooring in the basement is made from primarily natural raw materials, including linseed oil, rosins, and wood flour with a natural jute backing. It's installed with solvent-free adhesives and no VOCs. Forbo; www.themarmoleumstore.com

Windows and Doors
Low-E argon-filled thermally insulated wood-clad windows and doors help reduce energy consumption by reducing the amount of heat loss in the winter and heat gain in the summer. In addition, the windows keep UV light rays from the furniture and fabrics. Marvin: 888-537-7828; www.marvin.com

Hunter Douglas
www.hunterdouglas.com
The soft fabric panels rotate to control light and privacy. The roman shades are light-filtering alternatives to solar screens.

Radiators
Myson Decor Series panel radiators, column radiators, and hydronic towel warmer efficiently heat the home with warm, gentle, radiant heat and no sacrifice of floor space or aesthetics. Each radiator and towel warmer is controlled independently, so they can be turned off when not in use, enhancing energy savings. Myson: 800-698-9690; www.mysoninc.com

Glass Conservatory

The Ultra Living Collection vinyl Georgian conservatory, located on the roof, is Energy Star rated and uses Conservaglass glazing, which reduces the heat gain, glare, and UV damage with twice the insulating power. Four Seasons: 800-368-7732; www.fourseasonssunrooms.com

Roofing

GAF EverGuard TPO 80 mil Membrane protects the roof from water penetration. The white reflective color also reflects heat away from the house. GAF Materials Corporation: www.gaf.com

Green Roof

An extensive green roof requires little maintenance and helps manage storm runoff by absorbing rainwater. A green roof lowers air-conditioning costs, adds years to the life of the roof, and helps reduce pollution, including greenhouse gases. Xero Flor America; www.xeroflora.com

Rooftop water feature

Tudor Farmer, 310-621-8977
Tudor Farmer constructed a water sculpture for the roof made from recycled steel.

Indoor Floral Arrangements and Outside Window Boxes

Urban Flora, Steven Geldman, 212-260-0564
Steven Geldman also painted the landscape above the living room couch.

Kitchen and Bathroom Countertops

IceStone is made of recycled glass and concrete and is available in twenty-seven colors. It is heat resistant, as strong as granite, and free of volatile organic compounds. IceStone: 718-624-4900; www.icestone.biz

Kitchen Cabinets

Fabricated by Neil Kelly Cabinets: 503-335-9207; www.neilkellycabinets.com

Floor Tiles

Italian tilemaker Ragno has received certification for its environmental management program. The company also promises to eliminate harmful effects on the environment during tile production. Ragno: www.ragno.it

Kitchen Backsplash

The backsplash tiles are made from recycled bottles mixed with silica sand, a renewable resource. Oceanside Glass Tile; www.glasstile.com

Bathroom Tile

Atlas Concorde guarantees the sustainability of all processes used in production of their porcelain stoneware collections. Porcelain is an antiallergenic, durable material. Altas Concorde: www.atlasconcorde.com

Master Bath Faucets, Sink, and Shower

Lefroy Brooks, www.lefroybrooks.com
Thermostatic valves in the shower and bathtub prevent scalding and save water by allowing quick adjustment of water temperature, thus saving water. Lefroy Brooks ships its products in recycled packaging.

Master Bath Whirlpool Spa

Bain Ultra, www.bainultra.com
The Canadian company BainUltra makes baths that use air jets instead of water jets. Air jets prevent mold and mildew from accumulating inside a tub's inner machinery.

Powder Room, Boy's Bath, and Laundry Room Ceramic Tile

Imagine Tile, www.imaginetile.com
Imagine Tile pioneered the art of digital images in ceramic tile. Tiles are unaffected by sunlight, chemicals, heat, water, or wear.

In-Line Ventilation Fans for Bathrooms and Laundry Rooms

Broan, www.broan.com
Utilizing a proper means of ventilating noxious indoor air contaminants is so important to a healthy home.

Sustainable Fabrics

Angela Adams's mod fabric collection is made from 100 percent postindustrial recycled polyester. Angela Adams: 207-774-3523; www.angelaadams.com

Mattresses

Antibacterial foam mattresses wick away moisture and resist pilling, chafing, shrinking, odors, and mildew. The clean foam contains no BHTs and no harmful fumes or carcinogenic chemicals. Cover-est: 866-717-4580; www.coverest.com

Sustainable Furniture

Desiron produced the living room's sectional sofa without using formaldehyde or endangered woods. **Environment Furniture** uses eco-friendly reclaimed wood in all its products. They made the children's beds, master bedroom end tables, living room cocktail table, and living room console. **Furnature** produces furniture without chemicals, dyes, polymers, or toxins. Based on designs by owner and architect Paul Gleicher, they crafted the master bed, mattress, chaise, bench, and chair. Todd Oldham by La-Z-Boy lounge chairs and sofas are made with bamboo and faux woods.
Desiron: 212-353-2600; www.desiron.com
Environment Furniture: 323-935-1330; www.environment-furniture.com
Furnature: 800-326-4895; www.furnature.com
La-Z-Boy; www.lazboy.com/oldham

iDor Audio/Video Intercome System

Siedle, www.siedleusa.com

Decorative Lighting

YLighting, www.ylighting.com ·
Ylighing is the largest online retailer of high-end modern lighting. Their extensive inventory includes low-voltage monorail lighting, Title 24–compliant lighting, iconic design pieces, and hard-to-find imported fixtures.

Children's Bedroom Carpets

FLOR, www.interfaceflor.com
One of the world's greenest carpet manufacturers, Interface FLOR carpet tiles are versatile, practical, recyclable, and easy to install.

Light Fixture Supplier

MSK Illuminations, 212-888-6474
MSK Illuminations helps source decorative lighting that can accept compact fluorescent bulbs.

Dobberfuhl
NEWLYWED NEST

Heating System
The house uses a Bryant gas furnace and has two zones—sleeping and living—to allow for flexibility and savings in energy consumption. Bryant: 800-428-4326; www.bryant.com

Cooling System
The Bryant cooling system with Quantum Plus variable-speed air handler automatically adjusts its speed based on home's cooling needs for less energy consumption than a standard air-conditioner. Bryant: 800-428-4326; www.bryant.com

Tankless Water Heater
Standard 40- to 50-gallon tanks use up tons of excess energy heating and reheating the tank to keep it hot all day. But tankless water heaters instantly heat water only on demand, using less energy and saving money. Noritz: 866-766-7489; www.noritz.com

Windows
Double-gazed windows with low-E coating provide maximum energy efficiency and limited UV gain. Kolbe & Kolbe: www.kolbe-kolbe.com

Structurally Insulated Panels
SIPs reduce the home's energy needs significantly because the walls are one complete unit that includes an airtight insulating foam core. Another plus, there is no need for wood framing, additional insulation, or plaster. Premier Building Systems: www.premier-industries.com/pbs

Dual-Flush Toilets
Toto Ultramax dual-flush use 0.9 gallons or 1.6 gallons per flush. Toto: www.totousa.com

Washing Machine
The Energy Star Whirlpool front-loading washing machine and gas dryer uses less energy than conventional appliances. Whirlpool: www.whirlpool.com

Dishwasher
Their energy Star–rated dishwasher boasts significant energy reduction. Bosch: www.boschappliances.com

Low-Flow Showerhead
The master bath conserves water with Hans Grohe Croma EcoAIR 1-Jet showerhead, which uses air injection technology for a 1.6 GPM (gallons per minute) flow that according to the manufacturer feels like 2.5 GPM yet conserves water. Hans Grohe: 800-488-8119; www.hansgrohe-usa.com

Ceiling Fans
Ceiling fans lower the dependency on air-conditioning and circulate air for better air quality. In addition, the Modern Fan Company ceiling fan (guest BR) and Minka ceiling fan have dimmable light. Minka: 951-735-9220; www.minkagroup.net; Modern Fan Company: www.modernfan.com

Ennis
OCEAN BREEZE

Solar Panels
Fourteen south-facing solar panels convert the sun's energy into electricity for the house. Panasonic Photo Electric Panels: http://panasonic.co.j p/mesc/products/en/index.html

Structurally Insulated Panels
Prefabricated refrigeration SIPs with a high insulation value were used for the exterior walls, eliminating the need for wood framing and additional insulation. MeTecno API: 209-531-9091

Radiant-Heat Flooring
Two zones on each floor allow for targeted heating. Hot water, provided by solar collectors on the roof, runs underneath concrete floors that evenly conduct the heat. Acme Environmental Group: 310-397-2199

Boiler
An energy-efficient boiler provides additional hot water when needed with an extremely efficient system that burns 98 percent of the gas. Munchkin: www.radiantmax.com/r-munchkin-boilers.html

Kitchen Cabinets
The kitchen cabinets were made out of Forest Stewardship Council–certified walnut from a forest that practices sustainable growth. Through Cliff Spencer: 310-699-6013; www.cliffspencer.net

Appliances
The dual drawer dishwasher and the French door refrigerator are both Energy Star compliant, boasting energy and water savings compared to standard models. KitchenAid: www.kitchenaid.com

PEX Tubing
Instead of copper tubing, PEX tubing delivers water with better quality and purity. www.pexsupply.com

Pneumatic Elevator
The elevator is a prototype that is driven by electric motor. The cable is attached to an aluminum open crane that rides on plastic guides to keep the car from swinging on the cable as it goes up and down. N/S Corporation: 310-412-7074

Riili-Worton
THE ALLEY BOX

Insulation
R-23 blown cellular wall insulation is available through Gale Contractors: 360-403-1700.

Interior Paints
Benjamin Moore's Eco Spec paints are low odor and low in VOC (volatile organic compounds) for a healthier alternative to conventional paints. Benjamin Moore: 888-236-6667; www.benjaminmoore.com

Wood Finishes
Using water-based versus solvent-based finishes (lacquer, varnish) greatly reduces off-gassing and VOC. Sherwin-Williams: www.sherwin-williams.com

Salvaged Lumber and Brick
Using salvaged materials adds character to a house and is a wonderful way to recycle. The RE Store: www.re-store.org

Ceramic Tile Flooring
Ceramic tile is a nonallergenic flooring alternative.

Kitchen Cabinets
The cabinets are made of nonformaldehyde plywood with a rift sawn white oak veneer, not particleboard, so there is no off-gassing. Sky River Industries: 360-863-9888; www.skyriverindustries.com

Energy Star Appliances
Energy Star–rated appliances conserve energy and water.
Bosch dishwasher: 800-944-2904; www.boschappliances.com
Jenn-Air refrigerator: 800-jenn-air (800-536-6247); www.jennair.com. Frigidaire horizontal-axis washer and dryer: 800-374-4432; www.frigidaire.com

Sinegal
ROYAL RENOVATION

Biodegradable Cleaners
During construction, only vinegar mixed with water was used for a safe biodegradable cleaner.

Doormat and Shoe Racks
Because shoes track in a plethora of pollutants, the architects always add shoe racks and a doormat at the front and back doors, an easy way to prevent bacteria and viruses from entering the house. Custom through Stuart Silk Architects: 206-728-9500

Roof
A roof that is guaranteed to last at least forty years means less waste. Certain-Teed: www.certainteed.com

Energy Star Appliances
The dishwasher and microwave are Energy Star compliant, providing water and energy savings compared to standard models. Bosch: www.boschappliances.com

Talib
PARADISE BY THE SEA

Lightbulbs
Compact fluorescent bulbs last up to ten times longer than standard incandescent bulbs and use about 75 percent less energy.

Kitchen Cabinets
The pressed wood kitchen cabinets contain no formaldehyde, so there is no off-gassing of harmful chemicals. Nolte Kitchens: 954-929-0889; www.nolte-kuechen.de

Dishwasher
The Energy Star–rated dishwasher conserves both energy and water. Miele: 800-843-7231; www.mieleusa.com

Cooktop
An induction cooktop, which heats only the pan, not the cooktop, saves energy. Diva de Provence: 416-256-2646; www.divadeprovence.com

Dual-Flush Toilets
Toto dual-flush toilets give the option of 0.9 gallons or 1.6 gallons per flush to conserve water. Toto: www.totousa.com

Comforter
Made from a natural down alternative that contains no chemicals, this comforter is 100 percent biodegradable. Lyocell: www.lyocell.net

Bed Linens
Made without chemicals or harsh finishing agents, the sateen linens are made from 100 percent organic cotton. Earthsake: www.earthsake.com; 877-268-1026

Solar Hot Water Heater
Located on the roof, the thermal conversion system provides all the hot water for the house. TCT Solar: 941-957-0106; www.tctsolar.com

Soybean Insulation
Chemical-free organic poured soybean insulation provides airtight insulation. ComforTemp: www.ecomfortemp.com

White Ceramic Tiles
Placed on the flat part of the roof, the tiles reflect solar energy away from the house, keeping it cool and reducing energy needs. Sealoflex: www.sealoflex.com

Metallic Roofs

On the sloping part of the roof, 24-gauge galvanized metal roofing reflects the sun, reducing heat gain. AEICOR Metal Products: 954-974-3300; www.aeicormetals.com

Moore-Breedlove and Anderson-Boyd
SIDE BY SIDE

Heating and Cooling System

Separate heat pumps for upstairs and downstairs allow owners to customize how they heat and cool the house to be more energy efficient. Carrier heat pumps utilize a freon-free coolant (Puron) and improve indoor air quality. Carrier: 800-CARRIER (800-227-7437); www.residential.carrier.com

Tanklett Water Heater

The thermal reclamation unit uses heat produced by the air-conditioning system to preheat water. Rinnai; www.rinnai.us

Paints

Both units are painted with Sherwin-Williams no-VOC paints that reduce off-gassing and contribute to higher indoor air quality. Sherwin-Williams: www.sherwin-williams.com

Structural Frame

The structural frame utilizes recycled finger-jointed lumber as well as manufactured wood products, such as Timberstrand's LVLs, Glu-lams, and Parallam PSL to reduce the need for large whole trees. iLevel by Weyerhaeuser: 888-ilevel8 (888-453-8358); www.trusjoist.com

Dual-Flush Toilets

Toto dual-flush toilets give the option of 0.9 gallons or 1.6 gallons per flush to conserve water. Toto: www.totousa.com

Windows

All windows are high-efficiency, double-pane, low-E windows for maximum energy efficiency and limited UV gain. Don Young & Co.: www.donyoungwindows.com

Carpeting

InterfaceFLOR is an environmentally conscious division of FLOR that is working to reduce all their negative impact on the planet by the year 2020. The carpet tiles have a high recycled content. They are washable and can be replaced individually, if necessary, so your carpet has a longer lifespan. And when you're ready for something new, simply send the tiles back to the company for recycling. FLOR: www.flor.com

Ceiling Fans

Ceiling fans lower the dependency on air-conditioning and circulate air for better air quality. Monte Carlo: 800-519-4092; www.montecarlofans.com

Kitchen Cabinets

The wood in all IKEA cabinets comes from sustainably harvested forests. IKEA: www.ikea.com

Dishwasher and Refrigerator

Energy Star–rated KitchenAid S series uses less energy than standard dishwashers. KitchenAid: 800-339-6889; www.kitchenaid.com

Bennett
SIMPLY MODERN

Exterior Siding

Fiber cement board is termite and pest resistant and won't shrink or swell. The fiber cement board will not need to be painted for fifteen to twenty years and is guaranteed to last fifty years. The cellulose used in it is from plantation-grown trees and recycled wood pulp. James Hardie: 888 542-7343; www.jameshardie.com

Roof

The roof shingles are polymeric rubber designed to provide the look and feel of natural stone slate. They have a fifty-year warranty. EcoStar: 800-211-7170; www.premiumroofs.com

Rainhandlers

Instead of gutters, the house uses Rainhandler, a rain-dispersal system designed by engineers at MIT that directs rain away from the house. There is no need for gutters, and no erosion associated with the water coming off the house. Rainhandler: 800-942-3004; www.rainhandler.com

FSC-Certified Wood

Josh Jacobs, based in North Easton, Massachusetts, built the stairs from mapled certified by the Forest Stewardship Council.

Bathroom Counters and Sinks

Lithistone is a nontoxic, magnesium-based mineral cement compound that is stronger and more durable than concrete. The manufacturers use only nonsynthetic mineral pigments and food-grade sealers. Lithistone Design: 970-799-0181; www.lithistone.net

Kitchen Counter

Alkemi, a recycled composite material made of primarily postindustrial scrap aluminum, is hard, durable, and mimics the look of granite. Renewed Materials: 301-320-0042; www.renewedmaterials.com/alkemi.html

Kitchen and Laundry Room Backsplash

Backsplashes in kitchen and laundry room are made up of small square recycled glass tiles. Mosaic Source: 562-598-3143; www.mosaicsource.com

Kitchen and Bathroom Cabinets

The IKEA kitchen, laundry, and bathroom cabinets are made from sustainably harvested wood. IKEA: www.ikea.com

Cabinet and Closet Knobs

The cabinets in bathroom, laundry room, and bedroom closets feature knobs made from recycled and recyclable glass. Carina Works: 800-504-5095; www.carinaworks.com

Showerheads

The low-flow showerheads release 1.375 gallons per minute, which is significantly lower than the standard 2.5 gallons per minute. Bricor: 830-624-7228; www.bricor.com

Wood Floors

Lyptus is a hybrid of the eucalyptus tree that matures in just fourteen to sixteen years. Lyptus is a renewable, high-yield hardwood that comes from fast-growing trees on managed plantations that dedicate one-third of the area to the preservation of native vegetation and intersperse indigenous trees to preserve the natural habitat.
Weyerhaeuser: 800-525-5440; http://www.weyerhaeuser.com /ourbusinesses/buildingproducts/ buildingmaterials/ourproducts/lyptus

Icynene Insulation

Icynene is a water-blown policynene formula that forms a foam blanket with no air gaps, making it a very efficient insulator. It has no VOCs and no formaldehyde, producing a draft-free, noise-free, and allergen and pollution-free environment. Icynene: 800-758-7325; http://www.icynene.com

Plaster and Natural Tints

The all-natural-tinted plaster requires no paint and is completely nontoxic. American Clay uses natural clays, recycled and reclaimed aggregates, and natural pigments. The clays are nondusting, mold and fade resistant, repairable, and moisture controlling. Because the clay breathes, the walls humidify in dry conditions and dehumidify in moist conditions. American Clay: 866-404-1634; www.americanclay.com

Waterless Urinal

The waterless urinal works completely without water or flush valves. The system is touch free, improves restroom sanitation, and eliminates odors. Waterless: 888-663-5874; www.waterless.com

Dual-Flush Toilets

Toto dual-flush toilets give the option of 0.9 gallons or 1.6 gallons per flush to conserve water. Toto: www.totousa.com

Ceiling Fans

All the ceiling fans in the house are Hampton Bay Gossamer Wind Series fans with blades designed by an aeronautical engineer, and they consume approximately half the energy of conventional ceiling fans. Hampton Bay: www.hamptonbayinfo.com

Indoor Light Fixtures

All sconces and hanging pendants are made from 100 percent postindustrial recycled acrylic and use compact fluorescent bulbs. The chandelier is also made from 100 percent recycled scrap aluminum by CP lighting. All recessed lights, throughout the house, upstairs and down, are LED fixtures from PermLight and use 30 percent less energy than fluorescent. Permalight: www.cplighting.com; www.permlight.com

Appliances

LG Electronics, model WM2042C (washing machine), and matching dryer. The energy-efficient washer uses 252 kWh/year. The electric dryer is powered by a solar panel. LG: www.lge.com
Asko Dishwasher, model D3531XLFI, uses only 194 kWh/year.
Asko: www.askousa.com
Kenmore, model 74203, refrigerator, Energy Star rated, uses only 417kWh per year. Kenmore: www.kenmore.com
The Peerless Premiere gas range is the only gas stove that does not have an electric burner bar or a pilot light, thus reducing both electricity and gas consumption. Peerless: 312-602-2652; http://www.peerlessstoves.com

McMurtrie-Service
SUN HOME

Dimmer Switches

Using dimmer switches allows you to use only the exact amount of light needed, lowering energy use. Lutron: 888-LUTRON1 (888-588-7661); www.lutron.com

Boiler

A gas-fired high-efficiency boiler is 98 percent efficient.
Viessmann: 800-387-7373; www.viessmann-us.com

Ventilator

The Lifebreath Heat Recovery Ventilator provides fresh air from the outside that has been tempered with outgoing stale indoor air.
Lifebreath: www.lifebreath.com

Windows

All windows in the house feature a low-E coating that reduces the amount of UV rays entering the home.
Vetter: www.vetterwindows.com

Insulation

As an alternative to conventional insulation that carries chemicals like formaldahyde, the insulation is made entirely from recycled newspapers. Nu-wool: 800-748-0128; www.nuwool.com

Foundation

The Superior Walls insulated precast concrete foundation is a more energy-efficient alternative to a standard concrete foundation. Superior Walls: 800-452-9255; www.superiorwalls.com

Water Heater
The GE SmartWater Heater is high-efficiency and vents through the side wall of the house. General Electric: www.geappliances.com/smartwater

Fans
A combination of a whole-house fan with smaller ceiling fans circulates air throughout the house.
Grainger: www.grainger.com
Hampton Bay: www.gossamerwind.com

Steel Siding
MBCI steel siding is made from partially recycled steel and is a recyclable product. MBCI: www.mbci.com

Outdoor Deck
The deck is made out of Bear Board, 100 percent recycled plastic (HDPE). Engineered Plastic Systems—Bear Board: 847-289-8383; www.epsplasticlumber.com

Appliances
All appliances are Energy Star rated and save water and electricity.
Frigidaire stove, washer, and dryer: www.frigidaire.com
Bosch dishwasher: www.bosch.com
Amana refrigerator: www.amana.com

Low-Flow Toilets
Low-flow toilets offer two flushing options to save water.
Kohler: www.kohler.com

Goldberg
FROM THE ASHES

Radiant-Heat Flooring
Natural gas–fired hydronic heating warms up the floor, eliminating many air quality issues associated with ductwork, such as dust and mold. Radiant Tech: 425-402-8874; www.affordableheat.com

Cistern
The 85-gallon cistern collects rainwater, which is then reused for watering the lawn and plantings.
NW Dreamscapes: 360-424-0356; www.rainbarrelsconserve.com

Interior Paint
Benjamin Moore's Eco Spec paints are low odor and low in VOCs (volatile organic compounds) for a healthier alternative to conventional paints.
Benjamin Moore: 888-236-6667; www.benjaminmoore.com

Wood Finish
AFM Safecoat Polyureseal finish is a water-based clear-gloss finish that is low in VOCs and low odor. AFM Safecoat: 800-239-0321; www.afmsafecoat.com

Floor Finish
OS Hardwax Oil is a vegetable oil–based natural wood sealant that forms a waterproof finish on porous surfaces such as bamboo and cork. Available through www.ecoproducts.com

Bamboo Floor
Bamboo is a renewable resource that matures in three to five years and provides a durable, long-lasting alternative to tropical hardwoods. Vertical grain bamboo floors are available in a variety of stains. Timbergrass: 800-929-6333; www.teragren.com

Metal Roof
Custom-fabricated zincalume metal roofing is highly durable and helps reduce heat gain.
Marvin Sheet Metal: 253-752-5055.

Subflooring
The plywood subflooring is FSC-certified that it comes from a sustainably managed forest.
The Home Depot: 800-553-3199; www.thehomedepot.com

Insulation
The batt insulation is formaldehyde free to limit off-gassing.
Johns Manville: 800-654-3103; www.johnsmanville.com

Ceiling Fans
Ceiling fans lower the dependency on air-conditioning and circulate air for better air quality. Modern Fan Company: 888-588-3267; www.modernfan.com

Concrete Floor
High-volume fly ash concrete floors use fly ash, a by-product of coal-burning power plants that usually ends up in a landfill, mixed with the concrete to make it stronger and more water resistant. These floors were fixed with 50 percent fly ash. Salmon Bay Sand and Gravel: 206-784-1234; www.sbsg.com

Dishwasher
The Energy Star–rated dishwasher boasts significant energy reduction. Bosch: 800-944-2904; www.boschappliances.com

Dual-Flush Toilet
Caroma's dual-flush toilet offers a choice of 0.8 or 1.6 gallons per flush to conserve water. Caroma: 604-538-7677; www.caromausa.com

Cork Floor
Natural cork tiles are a renewable material and soft underfoot. Gerbert: 800-828-9461; www.gerbertltd.com

Carpet Tiles
InterfaceFLOR is an environmentally conscious division of FLOR that is working to reduce all their negative impact on the planet by the year 2020. The carpet tiles have a high recycled content. They are washable and can be replaced individually, if necessary, so your carpet has a longer lifespan. When you're ready for something new, simply send the tiles back to the company for recycling. FLOR: www.flor.com

Skillman
CLIFF DWELLERS

Heating System

A superinsulated water tank with a very high-efficiency condensing furnace saves energy while providing hot water needs for the house and the radiant heat floors.
Munchkin boiler: www.radiantmax.com/r.munchkin-boilers.html
SuperStor: http://www.jupiterheating.com/superstor-ultra-indirect-water-heater.html

Fans

Fans are a low energy alternative to air-conditioning. Windows placed to maximize cross-ventilation combined with ceiling fans help circulate the air throughout the house. Modern Fan Company: www.modernfan.com

Sod Roof

The sod roof helps keep the house cool by adding a layer of insulation and also extends the life of the roof. Janet Bell and Associates: 650-328-3400;
http://www.janetbellassociates.com

Bamboo Stairs, Side Tables, Bed, and Kitchen Cabinets

Bamboo is a renewable resource that matures in three to five years and provides a longlasting alternative to tropical hardwoods. Homeowner Peter Skillman crafted the master bed and side tables from bamboo as well. Plyboo: 866-835-9859; www.plyboo.com

LED Lighting

LEDs use about one-thirteenth of the energy of a standard bulb and 40 percent less energy than compact fluorescents and can last up to 50,000 hours. The Skillmans use LED MR16s and Par20s. Luxeon: 347-223-5077; http://www.luxeonstar.com

Dual-Flush Toilets

Toto dual-flush toilets give the option of 0.9 gallons or 1.6 gallons per flush to conserve water. Toto: www.totousa.com

Appliances

All appliances are Energy Star rated and use less water and energy than standard appliances.
KitchenAid Side-by-Side Architect Series II refrigerator: www.kitchenaid.com
KitchenAid Fully Visible Console Architect Series dishwasher : www.kitchenaid.com

Cork Flooring

Natural cork tiles are soft underfoot and a renewable material. Wicanders: www.wicanders.com

Seydel
ECOMANOR

Insulation

Cellulose insulation is made primarily from recycled newspapers. The highly effective insulator seals the home against air infiltration to maximize energy efficiency. Cellulose Insulation Manufacturers Association: 888-881-2462; www.cellulose.org

Flooring

The hardwood pine floors are from Avalon Plantation, a certified forest located in north Florida, part of the Turner Endangered Species Fund and certified by the Forest Stewardship Council. FSC: www.fscus.org.

Floor Stain

AFM Safecoat DuroStain has high adhesion and superior protection for porous surfaces and contains no aromatic solvents and no formaldehyde. AFM Safecoat: 619-239-0321; www.afmsafecoat.com

Rugs

The rugs are handmade with natural fibers and vegetable dye. Rugs by Robinson: 404-364-9042; www.rugsbyrobinson.com

Craftroom Flooring

Forbo Marmoleum flooring is made from primarily natural raw materials, including linseed oil, rosins, and wood flour with a natural jute backing. It's installed with solvent free adhesives and no VOCs. Forbo: www.forbo-flooring.com

Carpets (Lower Level)

Natural Elements is a collection of carpets and rugs made from sisal, coir, seagrass, mountain grass, and wool. Natural Elements Wool Carpeting: 800-843-1728; www.natural-elements.net

Solar Panels

Solar panels convert the sun's energy into electricity to support the home's energy usage. One World Sustainable: 912-898-9365; www.oneworldsec.com

Rainwater Collection

Rainwater is collected in large cisterns and used for flushing the toilets and irrigating the landscape. RainHarvest Company: 770-979-3380; www.rainharvestcompany.com

Gray Water System

Gray water is any water that has been used in the home, except water from toilets. Dish, shower, sink, and laundry water compose 50 to 80 percent of residential "waste" water that could be reused for other purposes, especially landscape irrigation.
Wade Plumbing: 770-461-6829.

Geothermal Heating
Geothermal heat pumps use the stable 51-degree F. temperature of the ground to heat and cool the house. By choosing geothermal, one can reduce heating and cooling costs by up to 50 percent compared with a conventional furnace and central air system. Geothermal systems deliver either forced air through ductwork or heated liquid through radiant tubing in the floor. Atlanta Gas Equipment Company: 404-761-2188

Computer-Controlled Energy Systems
A touch-screen computer system controls all the major systems in the house, including entertainment, security, communications, water collection, lighting, and climate control. Energy and water usage are observable minute by minute.
Interior Media: www.interiormedia.com
Lucid Design Group:
www.luciddesigngroup.com
Crestron: www.crestron.com

Doors
The Humabuilt Wheatcore interior doors have cores made of rapidly renewable resources with wood veneer exteriors. They are FSC certified, use ultra-low-VOC water-based adhesives, and contain no formaldehyde. Humabuilt: 541-488-0931; www.humabuilt.com

Countertops in Powder Room, Media Room, Craft Room, and Kitchen
Dex Studios mixes recycled materials such as mother-of-pearl, glass, and marbles with concrete to make custom countertops. Concrete is an eco-friendly alternative to nonrenewable natural materials such as quarried stone.
Dex Studios: 404-753-0600;
www.dexstudios.com

Appliances
Bosch's Energy Star–rated appliances boast significant energy and water reduction. Bosch: 800-944-2904; www.boschappliances.com

Kitchen Cabinets
Atlanta-based cabinetmaker John Bass is an expert in LEED certification standards and produces cabinets without chemicals by using renewable resources. The Custom Cabinet Shop: 404-350-8889;
customcabinetshop@gmail.com

Kitchen Cabinet Doors
Lyptus, a plantation-grown hybrid of the eucalyptus tree, matures in just fourteen to sixteen years and is produced in a sustainable and environmentally responsible manner. Weyerhaeuser: 800-525-5440; http://www.weyerhaeuser.com/ourbusinesses/buildingproducts/buildingmaterials/ourproducts/lyptus

Cabinet Boxes
With the growing focus on indoor air quality, Columbia Forest Products has produced a formaldehyde-free panel called PureBond, made from plywood, maple, and pressed hay and cost-competitive with standard hardwood cabinets. Columbia Forest Products: 800-237-2428;
www.columbiaforestproducts.com

Solar Tubing
All Velux solar tubing and skylights meet Energy Star guidelines and are 40 percent more efficient than most national building codes require. The glass used in the skylights and tubing provides great thermal protection, blocks all infrared heat and fade-causing UV rays, while letting in abundant natural light.
Velux: www.veluxusa.com.

Low-Flow and Dual-Flush Plumbing
Toto toilets and sinks optimize water conservation and provide consistent, exceptional performance. Innovations such as EcoPower fittings and valves, and highly active participation in and support of the United States Green Build Council (USGBC) make Toto an appealing option. Toto: www.totousa.com

Interior Paint
Benjamin Moore's Eco Spec line of paints are low odor and low in VOCs (volatile organic compounds) for a healthier alternative to conventional paints. AFM Safecoat also offers nontoxic paints and is able to match custom colors. Benjamin Moore: 888-236-6667; www.benjaminmoore.com; AFM Safecoat: 800-239-0321; www.afmsafecoat.com

Fabrics
All draperies within EcoManor were custom made from 100 percent natural fabrics, including cotton, silk, wool, linen, jute, and hemp. Fabric houses include: Grizzel & Mann, Henry Calvin Fabrics, Innovations, Nomi, Pindler & Pindler, Richard Bernard Fabrics, and Travis & Company.

Johnson-Chronister
UP IN THE TREETOPS

Cast Earth Construction
Popular in hot climates, cast earth construction eliminates the need for wood framing, thereby saving trees. The material also absorbs moisture, keeping the interior of the house cool and reducing the need for air-conditioning. www.castearth.com

Solar System
Solar panels convert the sun's energy into electricity. The 3-kilowatt photovoltaic system was installed by Andrew McCalla, Meridian Energy Systems: 512-448-0055; www.meridiansolar.com

Black Water Filtration
With the spray septic system, all of the water used in the house is treated and sprayed onto the yard, reducing the need for additional irrigation. HOOT Aerobic Systems: 337-474-2804; hootsystems.com

Insulation

The walls and roof are insulated with soy-based Cell-U-Insul spray foam, which expands to one hundred times its size, forming an airtight barrier that blocks mold, allergens, and noise. Because of the sealed thermal envelope, it takes less energy to heat and cool the home. BioBased Systems: 800-803-5189; www.biobased.net

Salvaged Doors

A local architectural salvage company provided all the antique doors in the house. Adkins Architectural Antiques and Treasures: 800-522-6547; www.adkinsantiques.com

Windows

Windows coated with low-E coating block heat and UV rays. Avalon Wood Windows: www.avalonwoodwindows.com

Paint

Benjamin Moore's Eco Spec paints are low odor and low in VOCs (volatile organic compounds) for a healthier alternative to conventional paints. Benjamin Moore: 888-236-6667; www.benjaminmoore.com

Ceiling Fans

Ceiling fans lower the dependency on air-conditioning and circulate air for better air quality. Minka: 951-735-9220; www.minkagroup.net.

Dishwasher and Refrigerator

KitchenAid Pro series dishwasher and refrigerator are Energy Star–rated appliances that use less energy and water than conventional appliances. KitchenAid: www.kitchenaid.com

Dual-Flush Toilets

Toto dual-flush toilets give the option of 0.9 gallons or 1.6 gallons per flush to conserve water. Toto: www.totousa.com

Stained Glass

All stained glass done by Lisa Chronister at Kali Studio: 512-789-3191.

McDonough-Trang
EXTRAORDINARY EXPERIMENT

Electric

The house uses off-site wind power from a nearby wind farm for all its electricity needs. Community Energy: 866-WIND-123 (866-946-3123); www.newwindenergy.com/

Heating and Cooling System

The custom hybrid system was designed by architect Michael McDonough. His Web site is interactive: www.michaelmcdonough.com

Bamboo Floors

Bamboo is a renewable resource that matures in three to five years and provides a durable, long-lasting alternative to tropical hardwoods. Plyboo: 866.835.9859; www.plyboo.com

Stainless-Steel Countertops

The countertops were custom-designed by architect Michael McDonough and fabricated in stainless steel, a durable, long-lasting material, by Elkay: www.elkay.com/

Bamboo Cabinets

Bamboo is a renewable resource that matures in three to five years and provides a durable, long-lasting alternative to tropical hardwoods. Fabricated by Artcraft: www.artcraftkitchens.com/cabinetconfig.htm; for Bilotta: http://www.bilotta.com

Appliances

All appliances are Energy Star rated and use less water and energy than standard appliances.
Asko dishwasher: 800-898-1879; www.askousa.com

SubZero refrigerator: 800-222-7820; www.subzero.com
Wolf dual fuel range: 800-332-9513; www.wolfappliance.com

Water-Saving Faucets

Water-saving faucets from Dornbracht's MEM line use aerators and other flow-control features.
Dornbracht: www.dornbracht.com

Dual-Flush Toilets

Toto dual-flush toilets give the option of 0.9 gallons or 1.6 gallons per flush to conserve water. Toto: www.totousa.com

Radiant-Heat Flooring and Cooling

Tubes carrying hot or cold water run under the floors throughout the house, providing heating or cooling when needed. PEX by Uponor Wirsbo: http://www.uponor-usa.com

Bedding

Organic bedding is free of all chemicals, made of 100 percent Indian cotton. Pure Rest Organics: 800-596-7450; www.purerest.com

Wente-Hyland
RURAL RETREAT

Solar Panels

Solar panels convert the sun's energy into electricity in this 3,240-watt active solar array. The inverter is connected to the local utility company. The Sharp 180 watt PV modules were purchased through Gaiam/Real Goods: 877-989-6321; www.gaiam.com/realgoods

Kitchen Cabinets
Kitchen cabinets are crafted from sustainably harvested chlorine-free anigre. Conlon Lumber: 914-946-4111

Appliances
All appliances are Energy Star rated and use less water and energy than their conventional counterparts.
Sub-Zero refrigerator: 800-222-7820; www.subzero.com
Wolf gas range: 800-332-9513; www.wolfappliance.com
Bosch dishwasher: 800-944-2904; www.boschappliances.com

Dual-Flush Toilets
Toto dual-flush toilets give the option of 0.9 gallons or 1.6 gallons per flush to conserve water. Toto: www.totousa.com

Lightbulbs
Compact fluorescent bulbs last up to ten times longer than standard incandescent bulbs and use about 75 percent less energy. Sunwave bulbs purchased through Gaiam/Real Goods: 877-989-6321; www.gaiam.com/realgoods

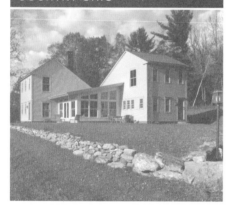

**Grier-Steckler
COUNTRY CHIC**

Foundation Sealant
A nonpetroleum-based product was used that provides a moisture-proof sealant for concrete foundations.
Rub-R-Wall: 614-889-6616, www.rubrwall.com/

Insulation
Nontoxic insulation is a combination of UltraTouch Natural Cotton Fiber insulation (www.bondedlogic.com/ultratouch.htm), cellulose insulation

(www.us-gf.com), and a Johns Manville nonformaldehyde product from www.jm-builder.com/products.php

Interior Paint
Benjamin Moore's Eco Spec paints are low odor and low VOC (volatile organic compounds) for a healthier alternative to conventional paints.
Benjamin Moore: 888-236-6667; www.benjaminmoore.com

Windows
All windows in the house feature a low-E coating that significantly reduces the UV rays that enter the home. They are double-paned and filled with argon gas for excellent thermal properties, reducing heat gain during hotter months, heat loss in the winter, and energy costs year-round. Marvin Windows: 888-537-7828; www.marvin.com

Radiators
A cleaner alternative to forced air heat, which encourages dust and mold, radiators are space-efficient and provide heat to individual rooms as needed.
Runtal: 800-526-2621; www.runtalnorthamerica.com

Wood Finish
Tung oil is an all-natural alternative to toxic wood finishes. It's derived from the nuts of the tung tree and provides a glowing, low-gloss, moisture-proof sealant. Sutherland Welles: 800-322-1245; www.tungoilfinish.com

Boiler
The gas-fired high-efficiency condensing wall-mounted boiler is 98 percent efficient. Viessmann: 800-387-7373; www.viessmann-us.com

Central Vacuum
A central vacuum cleaner improves air quality by reducing airborne allergens and dust particles. Beam Industries: www.beamvac.com

Living Room Chaise and Red Upholstered Chair
Mitchell Gold uses only wood that is certified from a sustainable forest. Cushions are crafted from nontoxic ozone-friendly foam.
Mitchell Gold: www.mgandbw.com

**Hughey-Clancey
WOODLAND HIDEAWAY**

AAC
Autoclaved aerated concrete is a concrete compound made by mixing aluminum powder and concrete. It's lightweight, soundproof, fireproof, bulletproof, and resistant to mildew. It uses very little cement and eliminates the need for wood framing and insulation. It has excellent thermal properties.
Manufacturer: www.Aerconfl.com
Available through Tristate AAC: 201-725-3563

Boiler
The furnace is EPA approved and very efficient, converting 98 percent of the gas into heat.
Peerless: www.peerlessboilers.com

Charcoal Stain
The concrete floors and the concrete counter were dyed with a charcoal pigment to give it the look of worn leather. Stampcrete: 800-233-3298; www.stampcrete.com

Wood Finish
The kitchen counter was sealed with a vegetable oil, available through Woodworker's Supply: 800-645-9292; www.woodworker.com

Natural Pigment
The walls were stained with all-natural, nontoxic pigments. Kremer Pigments: www.traditional-building.com/brochure.kremer.htm

Energy Star Appliances
All the appliances in the kitchen are Energy Star rated and use less energy and water than conventional appliances.
Amana; www.amana.com

ACKNOWLEDGMENTS

When we embarked upon this journey, we never knew which way the green brick road would take us, and it has been an exciting and memorable adventure that will continue for the rest of our lives.

We would like to acknowledge those folks who helped make the green dream come true. Linda Hall, Sara Bliss, and Amy Kaplan, whose respective genius with a camera, a keyboard, and an Excel spreadsheet cannot be underestimated. Not only were they talented and relentless in their ecopursuits, they were an absolute dream to work with on *Dreaming Green*.

Our agent, Larry Kirshbaum, is the epitome of class and style. Thanks for all you have done to help realize our vision and become a great friend along the way.

At Clarkson Potter, Doris Cooper, Lauren Shakely, and Amy Pierpont embraced this book in a personal and very wonderful way. And we thank Lindsay Miller, for all her constant attention to green detail and for keeping the project supremely organized.

And thank you to Michael Morrison, Jane Friedman, and Brian Murray at HarperCollins for believing a TV producer can have book sense.

Before we went green at home, we were inspired by a great couple who did it before us: Jim and Nancy Chuda. Their pioneering work and help with resources were invaluable. Carrie Cook, we thank you for making the introduction. The guest room is always here for you.

To Kelly Tagore, we'll never forget how you were so generous with your knowledge. To our early supporters at Hearst, Ellen Levine, mentor and true friend. Also Sean Sullivan and Richard Eisenberg, for their help pulling this project together. We also want to give a special shout-out to Jonathan Schein and the environmentally aware publishing team at the House Media Network for their help with selecting some of the truly special homes for this book and for believing in our mission.

Family means everything to us and we owe our parents a lifetime of gratitude. In particular, the late Norman Gleicher, who died too young from smoking: You remind us every day to keep our indoor air clean and healthy. To Mom and Art, Dad and Pat, Mom and Seymour, Nana and Jesse, thanks for never being critical, always going along for the ride, and being phenomenal grandparents and great-grandparents. To our siblings, Pamelah, Tina and Seth, Warren and Amy; and our nephews, Jon, Adam, Max, Jacob, and Charlie, we love you unconditionally. And to Eric Weinstein, cousin-brother, godfather, pillar of strength, you rock!

We are so very blessed with great support from Elaine Aguilar, who makes our home life run like clockwork.

At Gleicher Design Group, to the incredible and inspirational David Barry, for your interior design skill and patience. To John Graham and Nicole Gustafson, kudos for your talent and follow-through. To our contractor George Constant at Abigail Hess interiors, who met the very tight deadlines with grace and style.

To our dear friends Lori and Jacques for being our family through and through. To the healers who are true friends in our lives, Simon Taffler, Dennis Paulson, Ellie Crystal, and Frank Andrews. To Heide and Howard Lazar, Jessica and Drew Guff, for your friendship. To Diana Aldridge, always Lady Di to us, a great person and tremendous friend. To our friends at the Collegiate and Nightingale Bamford schools we are so grateful for the superb education of the hearts and minds of our sons and daughter.

To the leaders in the green movement, from His Royal Highness the Prince of Wales and Nobel Peace Prize–winner Al Gore to the awareness-raising groups, such as Environmental Defense and Global Green, we hope this book helps continue the mission you so passionately began.

INDEX

Page numbers in *italics* refer to photographs.

AAC (autoclaved aerated concrete) walls, 178, *180–81,* 185, 220, 222, 223, 236

Adams, Angela, *16,* 19–24, *20, 21,* 27, 227

air-conditioning, 228; heat recovery system for, 99, 230; minimizing or eliminating need for, 32, 42–47, 65, 83, 94, 106–10, 133, 145, 200, 201, 223, 233. *See also* cooling

Alkemi, 106, 111, *111,* 230

allergens, reducing, 27, 105, 110, 226

anigre wood, *191,* 196, 201, 236

antique furnishings, 150, *152, 157, 160,* 167–71, *170, 171, 196, 222;* beds, retrofitted to current sizes, *197,* 208, *211;* pairing with modern design, 204, *205,* 208

appliances: Energy Star, 89, 99, 171, 226, 228, 229, 232, 233, 234, 235, 236; salvaged, 68, 77. *See also specific appliances*

backsplashes, 19, *24–25,* 27, *27,* 227, 230

bamboo: cabinets, 140, *144,* 145, *180,* 185, 233, 235; flooring, 32, *32,* 97, 128, *175,* 185, 232, 235; furniture, *14–15, 56,* 60, *185,* 233; stairways, 145, *176,* 233

Barger, Jim, 57, 60, 225

barnwood siding, reclaimed, 119, 121

bathrooms: cabinets for, *37,* 53, *62, 144,* 230, 231; exposed piping in, *131;* IceStone countertops for, 19, *23,* 27, *27,* 227; Lithistone counters and sinks for, 230; master, *23, 33, 37, 45, 76,* 89, 97, *98, 99, 109, 111, 144, 156, 183, 190, 197, 210, 222;* pebble flooring for, 106, *111;* porcelain tiles for, 227; powder room, *26;* recycled glass tiles for, *23,* 27, 227; thermostatic valves for, 227; tubular skylights for, 39, *156,* 161; ventilation fans for, 227; water-saving fixtures for, 99, 173, *183,* 228, 229, 230, 231, 233, 234, 235. *See also* toilets

bed linens, 24, 229, 235

bedrooms, *118, 194, 197,* 220, *221;* children's, *22,* 24, *109, 118,* 129, *130,* 144, *156, 157, 158, 179;* flexible spaces and, 32–35; master, *23,* 24, *36–37,*

45, 60, *62–64,* 97, *108, 131, 134–35, 141,* 144, *151, 171,* 182, *182, 197, 211,* 220

beds, antique, retrofitted to current sizes, *197,* 208, *211*

Bennett, David, 57

black water systems, 171, 173, 234

Boeing jet, chairs made with metal recycled from, *56,* 60

boilers and furnaces: high-efficiency, 27, 53, 213, 223, 226, 228, 231, 233, 236; multi-zone systems and, 228

bricks, salvaged, 65, *65,* 229

cabinets: anigre, *191,* 196, 201, 236; bamboo, 140, *144,* 145, *180,* 185, 233, 235; bathroom, *37,* 53, *62, 144,* 230, 231; hallway, *115;* recycled glass knobs for, 231. *See also* kitchen cabinets

carpets. *See* rugs and carpets

cast earth construction, *166,* 167, *172,* 173, 234

cedar siding, *123,* 128

ceiling fans, 32, *108,* 110, 111, *114–15,* 133, *172,* 200, 201, *201,* 228, 230, 231, 232, 233, 235

ceilings: barrel-vaulted, *86–87;* double-height, *58–59,* 80, *122–23,* 127, *129;* salvaged, *56,* 57, 65, *65;* with visible joists, *144;* visually lifting height of, *74–75;* windows in, *189 (see also* skylights)

cellulose insulation, from recycled newspapers, 39, 121, 161, 209, 213, 231, 233, 236

chandeliers, *22,* 24, *74–75;* made of scrap metal, *102–3,* 106, 150, *152,* 231

charcoal pigment, concrete finished with, *221,* 223, 236

Chilcoat, Parrish, 47

Chronister, Lisa, 167–72, 235

cisterns, 161, 232, 233. *See also* rain barrels

clay walls, *8,* 27, 106, 110, 111, 226, 231

cleaners, all-natural biodegradable, 77, 223, 229

closet knobs, 231

closets, 226; tubular skylights in, 39, 161

Cobb, Chris, 29, 31–35, 225

color palettes, exterior, 140, 188, 196, 217

color palettes, interior, 24, 196, 220; black and white, 196; historical associations and,

171, 178; with jolts of primary colors, 81, *86–87, 94–95,* 97, *138–39,* 140; monochromatic, 128–29; neutral or earth tones with bright accents, *34–37,* 35–38, 60, *64;* New England light and, *207,* 208; primarily white, *71, 72,* 81, *86–87;* seasonal associations and, *146–47,* 149–50

comforters, 229

compact fluorescent bulbs, 171, 173, 229, 236

computer-controlled energy systems, 39, 161, 234

concrete, 89; in AAC walls, 178, *180–81,* 185, 220, 222, 223, 236; faux stone made of, *169, 173*

concrete countertops: embedded with vintage clock gears, 220, *223;* Lithistone as alternative to, 230; with recycled materials, *152–53,* 161, *161,* 234 (*see also* IceStone)

concrete floors, 57, 60, 99, 106; with appearance of stone, *216;* finished with charcoal pigment, *221,* 223, 236; with fly ash, 133, 145, 232; passive solar and, 65, 110, 111, 119, 121, *142,* 201; polished, *46,* 47, *48–51,* 92, 94, 97, *142;* radiant-heat, 110, *110, 116–17, 118,* 228; tinted, *39*

concrete foundations: with fly ash, 133, 145; insulated precast, 231; non-petroleum sealant for, 208, 213, 236; rubble trench as alternative to, 185

conservatory, rooftop, *14–15,* 24, 227

construction: AAC (autoclaved aerated concrete) walls, 178, *180–81,* 185, 220, 222, 223, 236; cast earth, *166,* 167, *172,* 173, 234; minimizing need for wood in, 89; structural frame in, 230. *See also* foundations

construction vehicles, disposal of oil and antifreeze from, 77

construction waste: recycling, 65, 77, 209, 213; reducing, *197,* 201

Cooke, Jillian Pritchard, 149–58

cooktops, induction, 229

cooling: cast earth construction, 167, 173; clay walls, 27; cross-ventilation, *61,* 73, 77, 110, 111, 133, *172, 189,* 223, 233; geothermal systems, 39, 161, 185; green roofs, 24, 27, 227; ground-level windows, 200,

201, *201;* minimizing or eliminating need for air-conditioning, 32, 42–47, 65, 83, 94, 106–10, 133, 145, 200, 201, 223, 233; radiant in-floor, *175,* 178, 185, 235; shade trees, *29,* 31–32, 133, 223; thermal windows and doors, 24, 226; thermostatically controlled skylights, 47, 53; ventilation systems, 32; venting through uppermost windows, *194,* 200, 201. *See also* air conditioning; ceiling fans; insulation

cork flooring, 106, *111,* 128, 133, *133,* 232, 233

countertops, *32,* 39, 140; cleared trees recycled in, *206–7,* 208, *208–9,* 213; IceStone, 17–19, *23, 24–25,* 27, *27,* 227; Lithistone, 230; with recycled scrap metal, 106, 111, *111,* 230; stainless-steel, 178, *180,* 235. *See also* concrete countertops

cross-ventilation, *61,* 65, 73, 77, 110, 111, 133, *172, 189,* 223, 233

curtains: natural fabrics for, 234; windows free of, 83, *104–5,* 105, *222*

decking, recycled plastic, *112–13,* 121, *121,* 232

decks and terraces, *67, 76, 112–13, 115,* 120, *132, 165, 190, 197;* on roof, 178, *182,* 185

dimmer switches, 111, 185, 231

dining areas, 19–24, *20, 21, 56,* 73, *74–75, 86–87, 90–91,* 97, *102–3,* 110, *116–17, 122–23, 127, 152, 160,* 191, *218–19,* 220; open layout plans and, *30–32,* 35, *38, 51, 136,* 150

dining tables, *20, 21,* 110, *152, 218–19,* 220; bamboo, *56,* 60; reclaimed-ash, *102–3,* 106, *110*

dishwashers, 228, 229, 230, 231, 232, 233, 235, 236

do-it-yourselfers, 124–29, 137–40

doormats, 77, 229

doors and doorways: arched, *168–69;* front, *30, 55, 71, 79, 216;* made with renewable resources, 39, *148,* 150, *158,* 161, 234; salvaged, 145, 167, 173, *173,* 235; sliding glass, *190;* thermally insulated, 226; without moldings, *34*

dryers, 228, 229, 231, 232

dust: curtains and carpets and, *104–5*, 105; heating systems and, 27; HEPA central vacuum systems and, 226

Eckmann, Jeff, 73
electricity: wind power and, 83, 97, 172, 178, 185, 235. *See also* photovoltaic panels
elevators, pneumatic, *46*, 53, 228
entertainment centers, 68, 73, *114–15*, 120
entry foyers, *37, 58–59, 71*, 73, *148*, 150

fabrics: child-friendly, 47; handcrafted by female artisans in India, 220, *221*; natural, 39, *68–69*, 150–58, *151, 157*, 161, *161*, 234; recycled, *16*, 19–24, *20, 21*, 27, 227
fans: ventilation, 227; whole-house, 73, 119, 232. *See also* ceiling fans
faucets, water-saving, *183*, 235
fiber cement board, 230
finishes: for floors, nontoxic, 213, 232, 236; low in VOCs, 133, 173, 185, 213, 229, 232; water-based, *62*, 65, 223, 229
fireplaces, 19, *53*; cast stone, 150, *154–55*; high-efficiency, *26, 184, 185*, 226; with salvaged materials, 217, 223
flooring: bamboo, 32, *32*, 97, 128, *175*, 185, 232, 235; ceramic tile, 227, 229; cork, 106, *111*, 128, 133, *133*, 232, 233; Lyptus, *8*, 24, 27, 106, *108, 109*, 111, 226, 231; Marmoleum, 39, *159*, 161, 226, 233; nontoxic stains and finishes for, 213, 232, 233; radiant-cooled, *175*, 178, 185, 235; radiant-heated (*see* radiant heating); for showers, *23*, 106, *111*; soapstone, *183*; with sustainable wood, 83, 89, 233; tile, *170*, 227; wide-plank cyprus, 167, *168–69*. *See also* concrete floors
floor joists, 226
fly ash–concrete mix, 133, 145, 232
Forest Stewardship Council (FSC), 196, 201, 213, 228, 230, 232, 233, 234
foundations: rubble trench, 185. *See also* concrete foundations
Freebairn-Smith, Rod, 137, 225
furnaces. *See* boilers and furnaces
furniture: bamboo, *14–15, 56*, 60, *185*, 233; with child-friendly materials, 38; custom-designed and -made, *23*, 24, *124–25, 129, 131*, 140; industrial chic and, *56*, 57–60; made of salvaged ship's hatch, *104–5*, 106; from previous home, reusing, 106, 120, 196, 201; with reclaimed wood, *16, 17*, 27, 227; with sustainably harvested wood, 208, 227,

236; vintage, 121; without toxic chemicals, *18–19, 23*, 24, 27, 208, 227, 236. *See also* antique furnishings

galvanized metal: roofing, 230; siding, 119, 121, *121*, 232
geothermal heating, cooling, and dehumidification, 39, 161, 185, 234
Gertler Wente Kerbeykian Architects, 188
glass, recycled: tiles with, 19, *23, 24–25*, 27, *27*, 200, 201, 227, 230. *See also* IceStone
glass conservatory, on roof, *14–15*, 24, 227
glass roofs, 44
Gleicher, Paul, 15–27, 225, 227
Goldberg, David, 123–33, 225
gray water systems, 39, 161, 201, 233
green roofs, *14–15*, 24–26, 27, *135*, 227
Gretter, Carol, 204
gutting process, 17

hallways, *44, 109, 115*, 120, *189, 210, 221*
hardware: recycled glass knobs, 231; salvaged, 68, 77, 167, 173, *173*
Harrison, William, 225
hazardous waste, disposing of, 17, 68, 77
heating: geothermal, 39, 161, 234; high-efficiency fireplaces, *26, 184, 185*, 226; multi-zone systems, 228, 230; pellet wood stoves, 110, 111; radiators, 27, 226. *See also* boilers and furnaces; passive solar; radiant heating
HEPA central vacuum systems, 226
Hertz, David, 42–47, 225
hot water: thermostatic valves and, 227. *See also* water heaters
humidity, reducing, 167, *170, 172*, 173, 185

IceStone: countertops, 17–19, *23, 24–25*, 27, *27*, 227; pavers, *14–15*, 26
Icynene insulation, 231
indoor-outdoor relationship, *189, 192–93*, 196
industrial chic, *56*, 57–60, *58–59, 61–65*
insulation, 106, 209, 232, 236; cellulose (recycled newspapers), 39, 121, 161, 209, 213, 231, 236; CertainTeed fiberglass, 226; Icynene, 231; prefabricated refrigeration panels, *40–41*, 42–47, 53; retrofitting, 68; of roof, 83, 89, 223; R-23 blown cellular, 229; soy-based, 89, 171, 173, 229, 235; structurally insulated panels (SIPs), 32, 228; windows and doors and, 226
invasive plants, 217, 223

Johnson, Elliot, 165–73, 225

kitchen cabinets, *86*, 227; anigre, *191*, 201, 236; bamboo, 140, *180*, 185, 233, 235; Lyptus doors for, 150, *152–53*, 234; nonformaldehyde wood products for, *61*, 65, 83, 226, 229; nontoxic water-based finishes for, 223; pressed-hay boxes for, 150, *152–53*, 234; salvaged, 167, *169*, 173; with sustainable wood, 17, *24–25*, 53, 120, *191*, 228, 230, 234
kitchens, 17–24, *24–25*, 68, *72*, 73, *86–87*, 97, *116–17, 118, 138–39*, 150, *152–53, 168–69, 195*, 206–7; backsplashes in, 19, *24–25*, 27, *27*, 227, 230; high-end chef's, 177–78, *180*; in open layout plans, *30–32, 34*, 35, *50–51, 56*, 57, *61, 64*, 94, *94–95*, 140; recycling center in, 140. *See also* countertops
knobs, recycled glass, 231

landscape irrigation: black water systems for, 171, 173, 234; gray water systems for, 39, 161, 201, 233; rainwater systems for, *30*, 39, 99, 121, 133, 161, 232, 233
landscaping and garden design, *121, 187*, 188, 196, *198–99*; container planting, *132*; invasive plants and, 217, 223; photovoltaic panel siting and, 196–200; protected during construction, 77
Lavacot, Kim, 57
LED lighting, 111, 145, 233
LEED certification, 106, 149, 234
lighting, *48–49*, 140, *145*, 227; compact fluorescent bulbs, 171, 173, 229, 236; dimmer switches for, 111, 185, 231; industrial chic, 57, *65*; LED, 111, 145, 233; reducing need for, 83, 89, *92*, 94, *95*, 99; tubular skylights, 39, *156*, 161, 234. *See also* chandeliers
light switches, *201*
limestone, *191, 195*, 196
Lithistone, 230
living areas, *16, 18–19*, 24, *26*, 47, 57, *68–69*, 73, *82, 88, 93, 95*, 97, *104–5, 107, 124–25, 144, 151, 154–55, 180–81, 202–3*, 204, *214–15*; entertainment centers in, 68, 73, *114–15*, 120; open layout plans and, *28–32*, 35, *48–49*, 150
local vendors and materials, 17, *191*, 196, 201, *210*
loft spaces, *62, 124–25, 126, 130*
long-life materials, 77
Lucas, Joe, 47
lumber: recycled wood products, 99, 230; salvaged, *64*, 65, 128, 133, *133*, 217, 223, 229
Lyptus, *158*; cabinet doors, 150, *152–53*, 234; flooring, *8*, 24,

27, 106, *108, 109*, 111, 226, 231

Marmoleum flooring, 39, *159*, 161, 226, 233
Mathews, Jonathan, 57
mattresses, 24, 227
McDonough, Michael, 187–201, 225
metal: roofing, 89, 230, 232; scrap, chandeliers made with, *102–3*, 106, 150, *152*, 231; scrap, countertops made with, 106, 111, *111*, 230; siding, 119, 121, *121*, 232
microwaves, 229

open floor plans, *30–31, 32*, 35, 94, 105–6, 119–20, *136*, 140, *144*, 150, 220

paints: low in VOCs, 24, 65, 133, 140, 173, 185, 208–9, 213, 226, 229, 230, 232, 234, 235, 236. *See also* pigments, natural
passive solar, 65, 115–19, 137, 209; concrete floors and, 65, 110, 111, 119, 121, *142*, 201; low-e windows and, 121; roof design and, 83, 89, *103*, 106–10, 111, 145, 185, 204, *212*, 213, 223; shape of house and, 110, 111, 119, 121; siting and, 83, 89, 110, 111, 119, 121, 178, 185, 204, 209, *212*, 213, 222, 223; window placement and, 65, 119, 121, 185
pavers, IceStone, *14–15*, 26
pergolas, *200*
PEX tubing, 53, 228, 235
Phillips, Liza, *18–19*
photovoltaic panels, 42, 53, 83, 111, 128, 144, 145, *147*, 172, 173, 178, 185, 201, 228, 233, 234, 235; siting of, 196–200
pigments, natural, *214–15*, 220, *221*, 223, 231, 236
plaster, tinted with natural pigments, *214–15*, 220, 223, 231, 236
plastic decking, recycled, *112–13*, 121, *121*, 232
plywood: birch veneer, *114–15*, 120; nonformaldehyde, *61*, 65, 226, 229
pools: infinity, *82–83, 134–35*, 137, 144; saline, 145
porcelain tiles, 227
porches, 89, *98, 215*; glassed-in, *192–93, 195, 198–99*
prefabricated refrigeration panels, *40–41*, 42–47, 53

radiant cooling, in-floor, *175*, 178, 185, 235
radiant heating: with hot-water radiators, 213, 236; in-floor, 53, 110, *110, 116–17, 118*, 121, 133, 145, *175*, 178, *183*, 185, 200, 201, *216, 221*, 222, 223, 228, 232, 235; in-wall, *189, 195*, 200, 201

radiators, 27, 213, 226, 236
rain barrels, 121, 133, 232
rain chains, *213*
rainwater: collection of, *30,* 39, 121, 133, 161, 177, *213,* 232, 233; directed to landscaping, 99; green roofs and, 27, 227; Rainhandler system and, 230
ranges, 231, 235, 236
Rashid, Karim, 140, *145*
recycled materials, 201; carpet tiles, *22, 24, 93,* 227, 230, 232; cellulose insulation, 39, 121, 161, 209, 213, 231, 236; chairs made with metal from Boeing jet, *56,* 60; concrete countertops with, *152–53,* 161, *161,* 234 (*see also* IceStone); containers made of tires, *58,* 60, *61;* fabrics, *16,* 19–24, *20, 21,* 27, 227; galvanized metal siding, 119, 121, *121;* glass knobs, 231; glass tiles, 19, *23, 24–25,* 27, *27,* 200, 201, 227, 230; plastic decking, *112–13,* 121, *121,* 232; rubber roofing, 106, 111, 230; scrap-metal chandeliers, *102–3,* 106, *152,* 231; scrap-metal countertops, 106, 111, *111,* 230; stone exterior, *147;* wood products, 99, 227, 230. *See also* salvaged materials
recycling, 140; cleared trees, *206–7,* 208, *208–9,* 213; construction waste, 65, 77, 209, 213; original house, 124, 133
redwood siding and interior walls, *28–31,* 32, 37
refrigerators, 228, 229, 230, 231, 232, 233, 235, 236
renovations, 15–27, 67–77
reusing and repurposing: furniture from previous home, 106, 120, 196, 201. *See also* salvaged materials
roman shades, 226
roof decks, 178, 182, 185
roofs and roofing materials: angled to minimize summer sun, *103,* 106–10, 145; glass, *44;* glass conservatory on, *14–15,* 24, 227; green, *14–15,* 24–26, 27, *135,* 227; insulation of, 83, 89, 223; long-lasting, 229; metal, 89, 230, 232; with overhangs to minimize solar heat, 94, 111, 145, 185, 204, *212,* 213, 223; passive solar and, *103,* 106–10, 111, 145, 185, 204, *212,* 213, 223; protective membrane for, 227; recycled rubber, 106, 111, 230; sod, 140, 233; water feature on, 227; white reflective, 83, 89, 227, 229
rubber roof, made of recycled material, 106, 111, 230
rubble trench foundations, 185
rugs and carpets, *18–19,* 133, 220, 233; FLOR carpet tiles, *22, 24, 93,* 227, 230, 232

salvaged materials: appliances, 68, 77; barnwood siding, 119, 121; bricks, 65, *65,* 229; ceilings, *56,* 57, 65, *65;* doors, 145, 167, 173, *173,* 235; hardware, 68, 77, 167, 173, *173;* kitchen cabinets, 167, *169,* 173; lumber, *64,* 65, 128, 133, *133,* 217, 223, 229; old ship's hatch, coffee table made from, *104–5,* 106; rain barrel, 121; stone lintels, 200, 201; timber, *56, 197,* 200, 201; trees, 188. *See also* recycled materials
Seydel, Laura, 148–61
shoe racks, 77, 229
showerheads, low-flow, 99, 173, 228, 231
showers, *23,* 89; flooring for, *23,* 106, *111*
siding, *120;* cedar, *123,* 128; fiber cement board, 230; galvanized metal, 119, 121, *121,* 232; prefabricated refrigeration panels, *40–41,* 42–47, 53; reclaimed-barnwood, 119, 121; redwood, *28–30,* 32
Sie, Susan, 217, 225
Silk, Stuart, 68–73, 225
sinks, *26, 131,* 234; salvaged, 68, 77. *See also* backsplashes
siting: for passive solar, 83, 89, 110, 111, 119, 121, 178, 185, 204, 209, *212,* 213, 222, 223; trees and, *29,* 31–32, 223
size of home, 32, 209
skylights, *44,* 140, *142–43,* 234; thermostatically controlled, 47, 53; tubular, 39, *156,* 161, 234
soapstone flooring, *183*
sod roofs, 140, 233
solar collectors: for hot water, 53, 83, 89, 128, 145, 229; for radiant-heat flooring, 228. *See also* photovoltaic panels
solar heating. *See* passive solar
solar tubing (tubular skylights), 39, *156,* 161, 234
sound absorbers, 105–6, *111*
soy-based insulation, 89, 171, 173, 229, 235
stained glass, *169,* 171, *171,* 235
stainless-steel countertops, 178, *180,* 235
stains, nontoxic, 233
stairways, *8, 37, 44, 46,* 71, *90–91,* 94, *96, 166, 170;* bamboo, 145, *176,* 233; crafted with scraps from lumber supplier, *58–59, 64,* 65; exterior, 178, 182; with industrial materials, *58–59, 64,* 65; Parallam treads for, *90–91,* 99, *99*
steel beams, 53
stone: bathroom walls, *144;* faux, made from concrete, *169,* 173; limestone, *191, 195,* 196; recycled, exterior made of, *147*
storage, hidden, *115,* 119, 120
stoves, pellet wood, 110, 111
structurally insulated panels (SIPs), 32, 228

stucco exteriors, 140, *145,* 222
studs, 226
subflooring, 226, 232
sun porches, *192–93, 195, 198–99*
sunrooms, *14–15,* 24, 68, *70, 72*

Talib, Kaizer, 79–89, 225
terraces. *See* decks and terraces
textiles. *See* fabrics
Thompson, Mary Ann, 105, 106, 110, 225
tiles: bathroom, *23, 27, 33,* 227; floor, *170,* 227; FLOR carpet, *22, 24, 93,* 227, 230, 232; porcelain, 227; recycled glass, 19, *23, 24–25,* 27, *27,* 200, 201, 227, 230; reducing construction waste and, *197;* from remainder bins, 200; white ceramic, on roofs, 83, 89, 229
timber, salvaged, *56, 197,* 200, 201
tires, recycled into containers, *58,* 60, *61*
toilets: dual-flush or low-flow, 99, 173, *183,* 228, 229, 230, 231, 232, 233, 234, 235, 236; rainwater collection for, 39, 161, 233
trees: cleared, recycling, *206–7,* 208, *208–9,* 213; dead, as indoor sculpture, *107;* recycled as pillars, beams, and railings, *164–66,* 173; salvaged, 188; shade, cooling and, *29,* 31–32, 133, 223; siting of home and, *29,* 31–32, 223
tubs, *23, 76, 183, 210;* Japanese soaking, 106, *183*
tubular skylights, 39, *156,* 161, 234
tung oil, 213, 236

urinals, waterless, 231
U.S. Green Building Council, 106

vacuum systems, central, 226, 236
ventilation. *See* cross-ventilation
ventilation systems, 32, 227, 231
Vicari, Tonino, 119, 225
VOCs (volatile organic compounds), paints and finishes low in, 24, 65, 133, 140, 173, 185, *208–9,* 213, 226, 229, 230, 232, 234, 235, 236

walls: AAC (autoclaved aerated concrete), 178, *180–81,* 185, 220, 222, 223, 236; clay, *8,* 27, 106, 110, 111, 226, 231; radiant heating in, *189, 195,* 200, 201; stained with natural pigments, *214–15,* 220, 223, 236
washing machines, 228, 229, 231, 232
water: black water systems and, 171, 173, 234; filtration systems and, 27, 226; gray water systems and, 39, 161,

201, 233; low-flow shower-heads and, 99, 173, 228, 231; PEX tubing for, 53, 228; water-saving faucets and, *183,* 235. *See also* rainwater; toilets
waterfalls, *173*
water features, rooftop, 227
water heaters, 226, 232; heat recovered from air-conditioners for, 99, 230; solar collectors, 53, 83, 89, 128, 145, 229; tankless, 228
Wedlick, Dennis, 204, 208, 225
Wente, Larry, 187–201, 225
whirlpool spas, 227
windows, 121, 178–82; argon-filled casement, *15, 18–19, 22,* 24, 226; available daylight and, 83, 89, *92,* 94, *95, 112–13, 115;* awning, *10;* casement, passive cooling and, 200, 201, *201;* in ceilings, *189;* cross-ventilation and, *61,* 65, 73, 77, 110, 111, 133, *172, 189,* 223, 233; energy-efficient, *104–5,* 230; floor-to-ceiling, *38, 52, 93,* 94, *95, 104–5, 107,* 110, *122–23, 127, 134–35, 141, 142, 190–93, 202–3;* free of curtains, 83, *104–5,* 105, *222;* indoor-outdoor relationship and, *38, 189, 192–93, 196;* with lattice screen to minimize summertime heat, *192–93, 195;* low-e coating for, 99, *99,* 121, 173, 228, 231, 235, 236; motorized gear system for, 47, *52;* passive solar and, 65, 119, 121, 185; picturesque views and, *42–43, 46, 66–67, 68–69, 76,* 83, 105, *109,* 144, 182, *182,* 188, *192–93,* 196, 204, *222;* with reflective solar film, *40–41, 45, 46,* 47, 53; roman shades for, 226; updating, 68, 77; uppermost, venting through, *194,* 200, 201. *See also* skylights
wind power, 83, 97, *172,* 178, 185, 235
wine cellars, *185*
wood: birch veneer plywood, *114–15,* 120; minimizing need for, *34,* 89; nonformaldehyde products, *61,* 65, 83, 226, 229; nontoxic stains and finishes for, *62,* 65, 213, 223, 229, 232, 233, 236; salvaged lumber, *64,* 65, 128, 133, *133,* 217, 223, 229; salvaged timber, *197,* 200, 201; for structural frame, 230; from sustainable forests, 111, *191,* 196, 201, 213, 227, 228, 230, 232, 233, 236 (*see also* bamboo; Lyptus). *See also* trees
Wright, Frank Lloyd, 178

Young, Travis, 91–97, 225

zincalume metal roofing, 232
zinc products, eliminating, 77